Scott Foresman

Imagine That!

Finding My Place

The Whole Wide World

Getting the Job Done

About the Cover Artist

As a child, Daniel Craig was crazy about dinosaurs, but in his Minneapolis home, his only pets are his cats, Isaac and Noah, and Winston, a dog. His pets often appear in his paintings.

ISBN 0-328-01817-1

6 7 8 9 10 V063 10 09 08 07 06 05 04 03 02

Scott Foresman Reading

Imagine That!

Program Authors

Peter Afflerbach

James Beers

Camille Blachowicz

Candy Dawson Boyd

Wendy Cheyney

Deborah Diffily

Dolores Gaunty-Porter

Connie Juel

Donald Leu

Jeanne Paratore

Sam Sebesta

Karen Kring Wixson

Scott Foresman

Editorial Offices: Glenview, Illinois • Parsippany, New Jersey • New York, New York
Sales Offices: Parsippany, New Jersey • Duluth, Georgia • Glenview, Illinois
Carrollton, Texas • Ontario, California

Unit 1 • Contents

Finding My Place

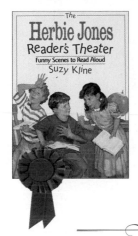

Unit 2 • Contents

The Whole Wide World

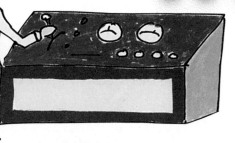

Unit 3 • Contents

Getting the Job Done

Janet Stevens

Dear Reader,

When I was growing up, I lived in many places because my dad was in the Navy. In third grade, I was the new kid . . . again.

My older brother and sister were straight A students. I was just okay at school. Good grades did not come easily for me. My older brother and sister were very smart. School seemed easy for them. I wanted to be smart. I thought I was not.

In third grade our class was divided into reading groups. The groups all had names: Cardinals, Robins, and Blue Jays. Cardinals were the best readers, the fastest readers.

We took a reading test to find out which bird we would be. I tried to read fast so I would be a Cardinal. But the story didn't make much sense to me when I read it that fast. "TIME'S UP!" said Mrs. Munsen.

Sometimes it's tough being the new kid. I felt as if I needed to impress everyone so they would like me. I needed to be a Cardinal. My stomach ached; my palms sweated. I thought, "Cardinals. Please make me a

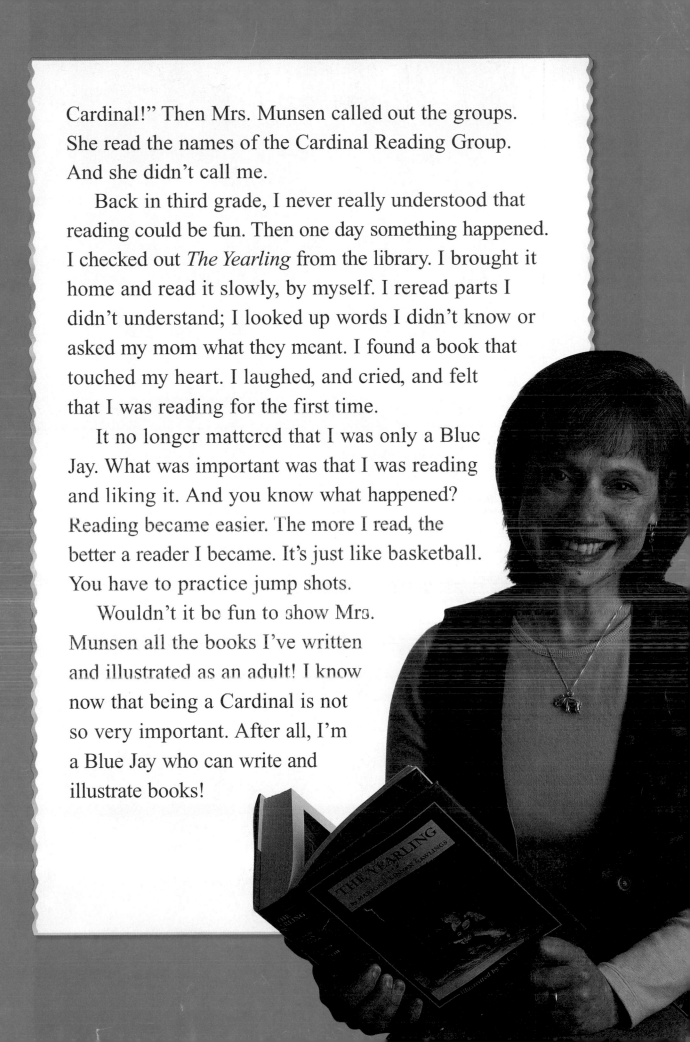

Cardinal!" Then Mrs. Munsen called out the groups. She read the names of the Cardinal Reading Group. And she didn't call me.

Back in third grade, I never really understood that reading could be fun. Then one day something happened. I checked out *The Yearling* from the library. I brought it home and read it slowly, by myself. I reread parts I didn't understand; I looked up words I didn't know or asked my mom what they meant. I found a book that touched my heart. I laughed, and cried, and felt that I was reading for the first time.

It no longer mattered that I was only a Blue Jay. What was important was that I was reading and liking it. And you know what happened? Reading became easier. The more I read, the better a reader I became. It's just like basketball. You have to practice jump shots.

Wouldn't it be fun to show Mrs. Munsen all the books I've written and illustrated as an adult! I know now that being a Cardinal is not so very important. After all, I'm a Blue Jay who can write and illustrate books!

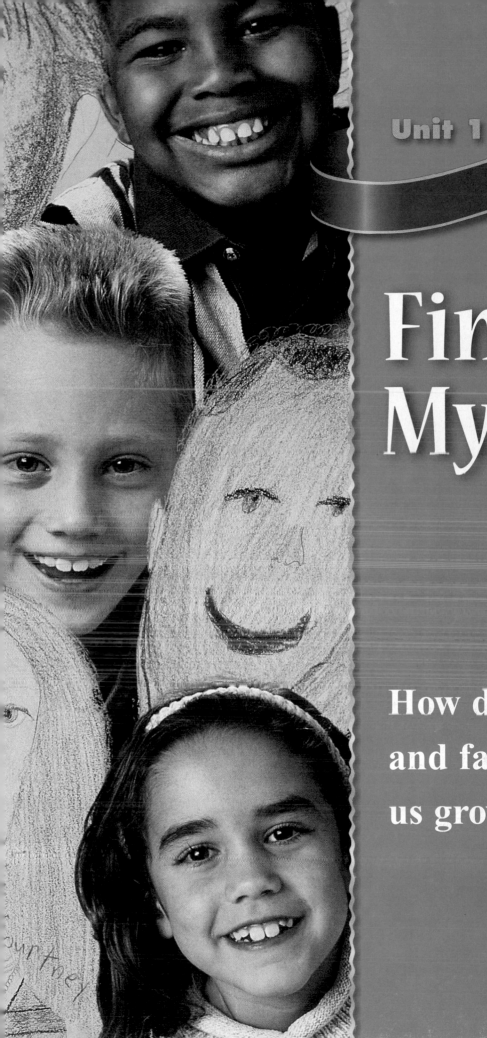

Finding My Place

How do friends and family help us grow?

Sequence

- **Sequence** is the order things happen in a story.

- Clue words, such as *before* and *after,* can tell you when something happens.

- Dates and times of day can also tell you when something happens.

- Picture in your mind what is happening. If the order does not make sense, try to figure out an order that does make sense.

Read "First Day at Camp" from *Arnie Goes to Camp* by Nancy Carlson.

Talk About It

1. When Arnie misses Louanne, what happens next that makes him not miss her so much?

2. When does Stretch take the campers on a hike? What clue words help you know this?

First Day at Camp

by Nancy Carlson

Arnie, who doesn't want to go to camp, has arrived with other campers for the first day.

When they arrived at camp, Arnie met his counselor Stretch. Stretch was eighteen years old and wore all sorts of camping gear on his belt. "Stretch is kind of neat," Arnie thought. When they all hiked to their cabin, Arnie thought of his mom. He felt like crying. Arnie's bunk-mate was a kid named Ted. Ted liked to play tricks. Arnie thought of his friend, Louanne. He missed her.

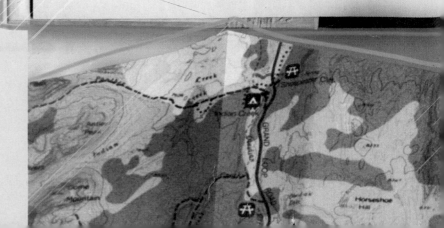

Suddenly a bell rang. "Oh boy, it's lunch!" yelled Ted. Everyone rushed off.

"I'm not hungry," thought Arnie.

But when Arnie sat down, he saw lunch was hot dogs and beans. "My favorite!" he said.

After lunch Stretch made everyone take a nap. "I'm too old for a nap," Arnie complained.

But all during naptime, Ted goofed off and made everyone laugh. "He's funny," thought Arnie.

After naptime Stretch told everyone to get ready for a hike. "I won't like this," grumbled Arnie. But the hike was fun. Arnie had never seen such neat things. He even held a snake.

LOOK AHEAD

In *How I Spent My Summer Vacation*, Wallace tells about his summer activities too. Read and tell the sequence of things that happen to Wallace.

Vocabulary

Words to Know

cowboys	imagination	summer
vacation	visit	west

When you read, you may come across a word you don't know. To figure out the meaning of the unfamiliar word, look for clues in the words around it. A clue can be in a description near the unknown word.

Read this paragraph. Notice how the description of *cowboys* helps you understand what it means.

A Trip to the Ranch

In my <u>imagination</u>, <u>cowboys</u> cook over fires after the long days of riding horses. Last <u>summer</u> when school was out, I went on <u>vacation</u>. On a <u>visit</u> to my uncle's ranch, I saw cowboys herd cattle, find a lost calf, and fix a fence. As the sun sank in the <u>west</u>, the cowboys did cook over the fire. But I felt lucky—I saw what their job is really like!

Talk About It

Tell a friend what you would like to do at a ranch. Use vocabulary words.

How I Spent My Summer Vacation

Written and
Illustrated by
Mark Teague

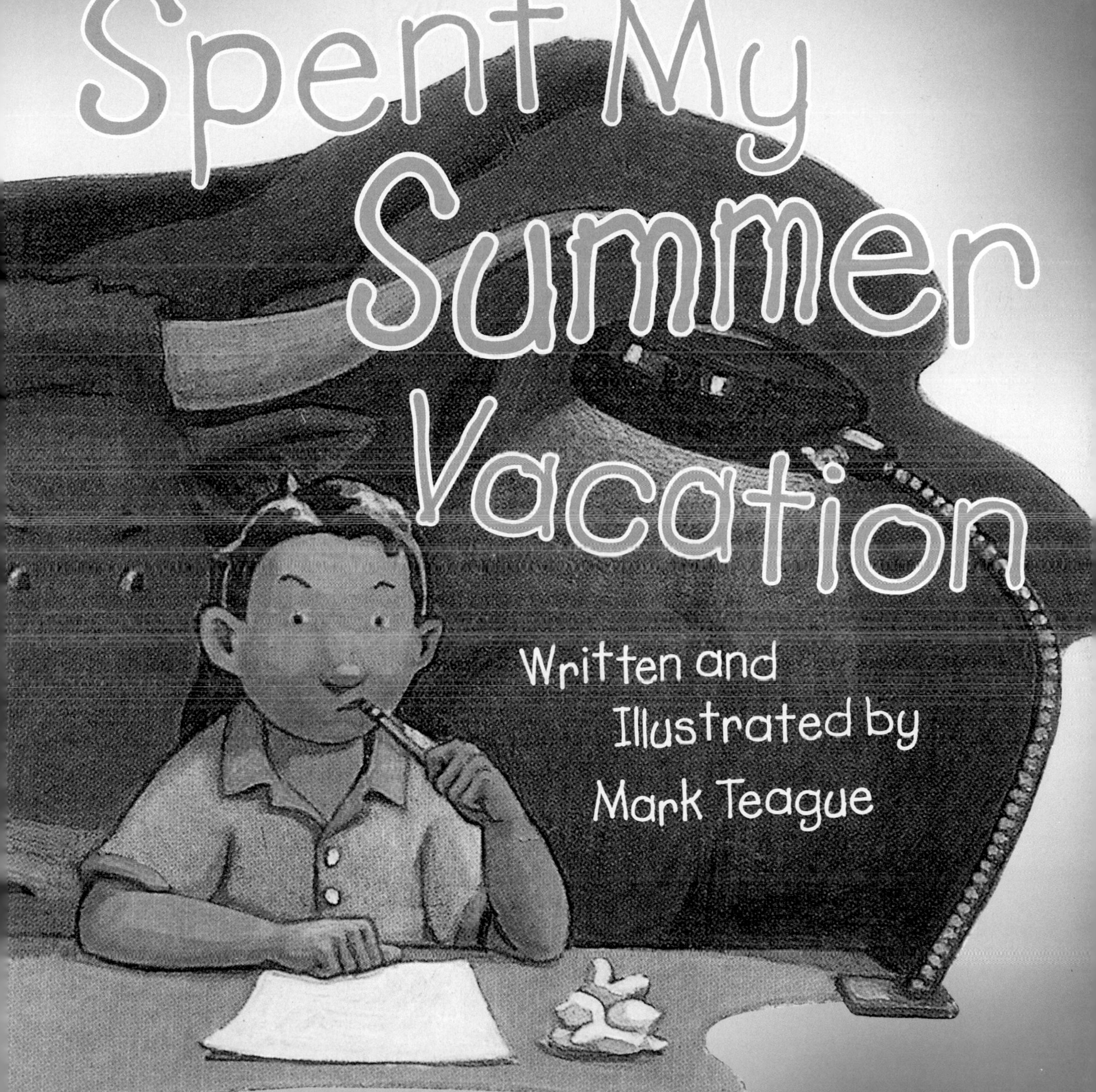

When summer began, I headed out west.
My parents had told me I needed a rest.
"Your imagination," they said, "is getting too wild.
It will do you some good to relax for a while."

So they put me aboard a westbound train
To visit Aunt Fern in her house on the plains.

But I was captured by cowboys,
A wild-looking crowd.
Their manners were rough
and their voices were loud.

"I'm trying to get to my aunt's house," I said.
But they carried me off to their cow camp instead.

The Cattle Boss growled, as he told me to sit,
"We need a new cowboy. Our old cowboy quit.
We could sure use your help. So what do you say?"
I thought for a minute, then I told him, "Okay."

Then I wrote to Aunt Fern, so she'd
know where I'd gone.
I said not to worry, I wouldn't be long.

That night I was given a new set of clothes.
Soon I looked like a wrangler from my head to my toes.
But there's more to a cowboy than boots and a hat,
I found out the next day
And the day after that.

Each day I discovered some new cowboy tricks.
From roping
And riding
To making fire with sticks.
Slowly the word spread
all over the land:
"That wrangler 'Kid Bleff'
is a first-rate cowhand!"

The day finally came
when the roundup was through.
Aunt Fern called: "Come on over.
Bring your cowboys with you."
She was cooking a barbecue
that very same day.
So we cleaned up (a little)
and we headed her way.

The food was delicious. There was plenty to eat.
And the band that was playing just couldn't be beat.

But suddenly I noticed a terrible sight.
The cattle were stirring and stamping with fright.
It's a scene I'll remember till my very last day.
"They're gonna stampede!" I heard somebody say.
Just then they came charging. They charged right at *me!*
I looked for a hiding place—
a rock, or a tree.

33

What I found was a tablecloth spread out on the ground.
So I turned like a matador
And spun it around.
It was a new kind of cowboying, a fantastic display!
The cattle were frightened and stampeded . . . away!

Then the cowboys all cheered,
"Bleff's a true buckaroo!"
They shook my hand and slapped my back,
And Aunt Fern hugged me too.

And *that's* how I spent my summer vacation.

I can hardly wait for show-and-tell!

Mark Teague

When Mark Teague was a
child, he loved picture books.
He especially loved writing and illustrating his
own picture books. As a young man, Mr. Teague
worked in a bookstore. While looking at the
picture books in the store, he remembered how
much fun he had when he made up his own
stories. He decided to write more stories—
and get them published this time.

Now Mr. Teague's stories and pictures
are in books that are read by thousands
of people. One thing has not changed
about the way he makes his books,
though. "I use a pencil for drawing
and a huge eraser for erasing until
I get it right," Mr. Teague says.

Other stories by Mark Teague
that you might enjoy include
The Trouble with the Johnsons and
Moog-Moog, Space Barber.

Reader Response

Open for Discussion

Imagine going on your own Wild West adventure. What would happen on your adventure?

Comprehension Check

1. Could any part of Wallace's Wild West story be true? Why or why not? Look back at the story to support your answer.

2. Look back at page 36. The cowboys call Wallace a "true buckaroo." What words from the story explain what the cowboys mean?

3. Wallace says he can hardly wait for show-and-tell. What do you think he means? Find evidence from the story to explain.

4. Clue words such as *first, next, last* or the time of day tell the **sequence,** or order, of events. List clue words in the story that tell when things happen. (Sequence)

5. Tell the **sequence** of events that happened to Wallace. (Sequence)

Test Prep
Look Back and Write

Look back at pages 21–36. Compare how Wallace feels when he is first captured by cowboys to how Wallace feels at the end of the story. Use pictures and details from the story to explain your answer.

The Picture Place

Myra Cohn Livingston

I drew a picture.
You and I
were underneath
a summer sky

but suddenly
you ran away.
I called and asked
if you would stay

but you had
left the page and stood
outside. You never
understood

I dreamed the picture
up to be
a special place
for you and me,

a place which no one else
had known,
where we could play
and be alone.

So come back in,
Step carefully
Into my picture place
With me.

Skill Lesson

Drawing Conclusions

- A **conclusion** is a decision you make about what happens in a story.

- Authors give details about what happens. They may give clues about why things happen.

- You **draw conclusions** when you use what you know to make decisions that make sense about characters or events.

Read "Spider's Story" from *Three Up a Tree* by James Marshall.

Write About It

1. After reading, write the word *chicken* at the top of a sheet of paper. Write two sentences about how the chicken feels and how you know this.

2. Share your conclusions with your classmates.

Spider's Story

by James Marshall

A chicken caught the wrong bus.
   She found herself in a bad part
of town—the part where foxes live.
   "Uh-oh," she said.

Quickly she pulled down her hat and waited for the next bus.

But very soon—you guessed it— a hungry fox came along and sat beside her.

LOOK AHEAD →

In *Goldilocks and the Three Bears*, Goldilocks does the wrong thing too. Read and get ready to draw your own conclusions about the characters.

Vocabulary

breakfast	forest	promise
comfortable	gobbled	
cozy	hungry	

Words that have similar meanings, like *hat* and *cap,* are **synonyms**. To find the meaning of a word, look for clues in words nearby. Sometimes the clue is a synonym.

Read the story. Notice how *snug* and *warm* help you understand *cozy.*

The Three Little Bears

Deep in the forest, three bear cubs were cozy in their bed, feeling snug, warm, and comfortable. But they wouldn't go to sleep. So Mother Bear told them a story: "Once upon a time, three bears missed their breakfast because they stayed up too late the night before. A little girl came into their house. She was so hungry that she gobbled up their breakfast."

The cubs said, "We promise to go to sleep."

Talk About It

Use vocabulary words to tell a friend your favorite tale.

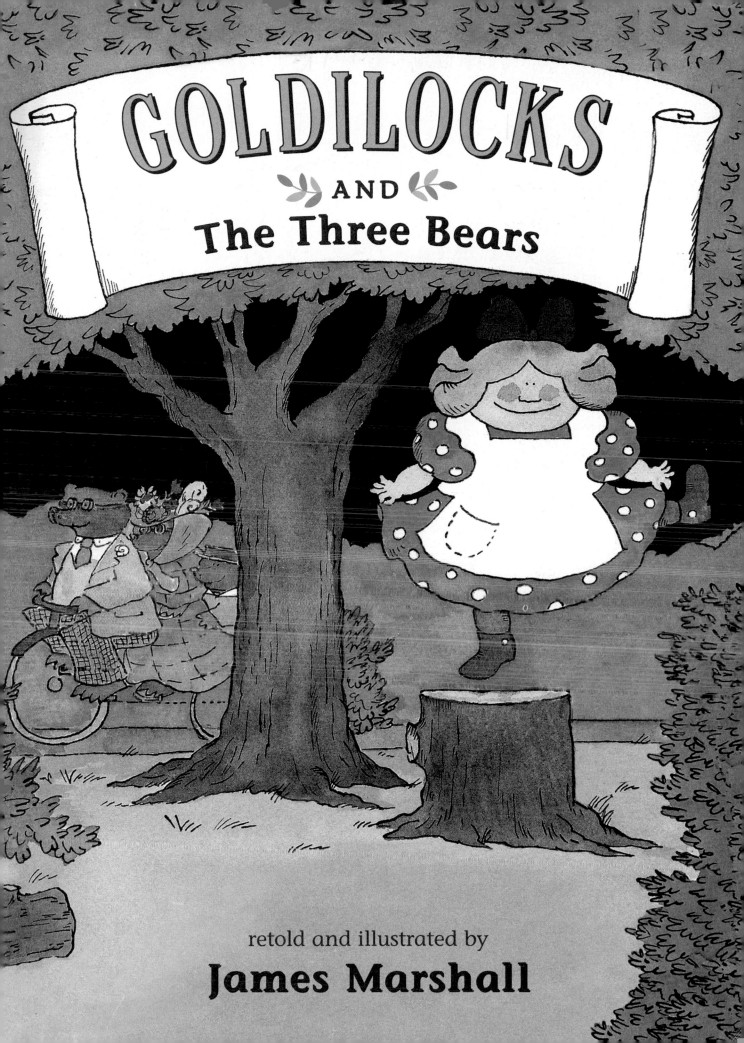

Once there was a little girl called Goldilocks.

"What a sweet child," said someone new in town.

"That's what *you* think," said a neighbor.

One morning Goldilocks's mother sent her to buy muffins in the next village. "You must promise *not* to take the shortcut through the forest," she said. "I've heard that bears live there."

"I promise," said Goldilocks. But to tell the truth Goldilocks was one of those naughty little girls who do *exactly* as they please.

Meanwhile in a clearing deeper inside the forest, in a charming house all their own, a family of brown bears was sitting down to breakfast.

"Patooie!" cried big old Papa Bear. "This porridge is scalding! I've burned my tongue!"

"I'm dying!" cried Baby Bear.

"Now really," said Mama Bear, who was of medium size. "That's quite enough."

"I know," said Papa Bear. "Why don't we go for a spin while the porridge is cooling?"

"Excellent," said Mama Bear. So they got on their rusty old bicycle and off they went.

A few minutes later Goldilocks arrived at the bears' house. She walked right in without *even* bothering to knock. On the dining room table were three inviting bowls of porridge.

"I don't mind if I do," said Goldilocks, helping herself to the biggest bowl.

But the porridge in the biggest bowl was much too hot. "Patooie!" cried Goldilocks. And she spat it out.

Next she tasted the porridge in the medium-sized bowl. But that porridge was much too cold.

Then Goldilocks tasted the porridge in the little bowl, and it was *just right*—neither too hot nor too cold. In fact she liked it so much that she gobbled it all up.

Feeling full and satisfied Goldilocks thought
it would be great fun to have a look around.
Right away she noticed a lot of coarse brown fur
everywhere. "They must have kitties," she said.

In the parlor there were three chairs. "I don't
mind if I do," she said, climbing into the biggest
one. But the biggest chair was much too hard, and
she just couldn't get comfortable.

Next she sat in the medium-sized chair. But that
chair was much too soft. (And she thought she
might *never* get out of it.)

Then Goldilocks sat in the little chair, and that
was *just right*—neither too hard nor too soft. In fact
she liked it so much that she rocked and rocked—
until the chair fell completely to pieces!

Now, all that rocking left Goldilocks quite tuckered out. "I could take a little snooze," she said. So she went to look for a comfy place to nap. Upstairs were three beds. "I don't mind if I do," said Goldilocks. And she got into the biggest one. But the head of the biggest bed was much too high.

Next she tried the medium-sized bed. But the head of that bed was much too low. Then Goldilocks tried the little bed, and it was *just right*. Soon she was all nice and cozy and sound asleep. She did not hear the bears come home.

The three bears were mighty hungry. But when they went in for breakfast, they could scarcely believe their eyes!

"Somebody has been in my porridge!" said Papa Bear.

"Somebody has been in *my* porridge!" said Mama Bear.

"Somebody has been in my porridge," said Baby Bear. "And eaten it all up!"

In the parlor the three bears were in for another little surprise.

"Somebody has been sitting in my chair!" said Papa Bear.

"Somebody has been sitting in *my* chair," said Mama Bear.

"Somebody has been sitting in my chair," said Baby Bear. "And broken it to smithereens!"

The three bears went upstairs on tiptoe (not knowing what they would discover). At first everything seemed fine. But then Papa Bear lay down on his big brass bed.

"Somebody has been lying in my bed!" he cried. And he was not amused.

"Egads!" cried Mama Bear. "Somebody has been lying in *my* bed!"

"Look!" cried Baby Bear. "Somebody has been lying in my bed. And she's still there!"

"Now see here!" roared Papa Bear. Goldilocks
woke up with a start. And her eyes nearly popped
out of her head. But before the bears could demand
a proper explanation, Goldilocks was out of bed,
out the window, and on her way home.

"Who *was* that little girl?" asked Baby Bear.

"I have no idea," said Mama Bear. "But I hope
we never see her again."

And they never did.

About the Author/Illustrator

James Marshall

James Marshall was a teacher who had a hobby. He liked to draw. One day a friend saw his drawings and convinced him to see a publisher of children's books. Mr. Marshall met with the person and the next day was asked to illustrate a book. Later he started writing stories to go along with the pictures he drew.

One time Mr. Marshall had a dream that a character in one of his books was upset with him. "She had become very cross with me. She wanted better stories, better lines!" The character told Mr. Marshall that if she didn't get them she was going to another illustrator's house!

Mr. Marshall's retelling of *Goldilocks and the Three Bears* was a Caldecott Honor Book in 1989. He also has retold the stories *Little Red Riding Hood* and *Cinderella*.

Reader Response

Open for Discussion

Some people believe folk tales teach important lessons. What lesson can you learn from this story? Explain.

Comprehension Check

1. On page 44, a new person in town says Goldilocks is a sweet child. A neighbor replies, "That's what *you* think." What does the neighbor mean? Find examples from the story to explain.

2. The pictures in *Goldilocks and the Three Bears* help tell the story. Find your favorite picture. Explain how it helps tell the story.

3. What do you think would have happened if Goldilocks hadn't jumped out the window? Use evidence from the story to explain.

4. Actions can help you **draw conclusions** about someone. What kind of girl is Goldilocks? Give examples of actions from the story. (Drawing Conclusions)

5. Now **draw conclusions** about Mama Bear. What is she like? Look back at the story to find support for your answer. (Drawing Conclusions)

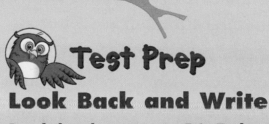

Test Prep

Look Back and Write

Look back at page 56. Baby Bear says his chair has been broken to smithereens. Use pictures and details on pages 52 and 53 to explain what *smithereens* means.

Test Prep

How to Read an Informational Article

1. Preview

- An informational article gives facts about a topic.

- Read the title and the first paragraph. Then look at the pictures. What is the topic?

2. Read and Make a List

- Read the article to learn facts about black bears. Then list the most important ones.

1. Black bears can climb trees.

3. Think and Connect

Think about *Goldilocks and the Three Bears.* Then look over your notes on *American Black Bears.*

Write a story about the Mama Bear, Papa Bear, and Baby Bear. Have them do something that real bears do.

Bear cubs enjoy playing, resting, and sunbathing in trees.

The black bear has short, curved claws, which help it climb trees.

If alarmed, black bears climb trees. A mother sends her cubs up the tree and then follows them or stays on the ground to face the danger.

American Black Bears

by Helen Gilks

American black bears are the most common bears in North America. They live in forests over much of the continent and are good climbers. Black bears are not always black; some are brown or even cream-colored.

Bears scratch themselves against trees. Sometimes they do this to leave scent marks to warn other bears, but sometimes just to relieve an itch from parasites such as ticks, fleas, or lice.

There are black bears with very pale fur on the west coast of British Columbia, in Canada. They are known as Kermodes bears, after the scientist who first described them.

In the heat of the summer, bears may cool off by lying in water. Black bears are excellent swimmers.

In May and June, when the hungry bears emerge from their dens, food is often scarce. Black bears will strip bark from trees such as the Douglas fir to get at the soft sapwood. One bear can peel up to fifty trees in a night.

Skill Lesson

Author's Purpose

- **Author's purpose** is the author's reason for writing.

- An author may try to inform, or explain something.

- An author may try to entertain you or let you have fun with the reading.

Read "A Cowboy's Rope" from *The Cowboy's Handbook* by Tod Cody.

Talk About It

1. What is the author's purpose for writing this? Why do you think so?

2. What things about a cowboy's rope did the author tell you that you did not know?

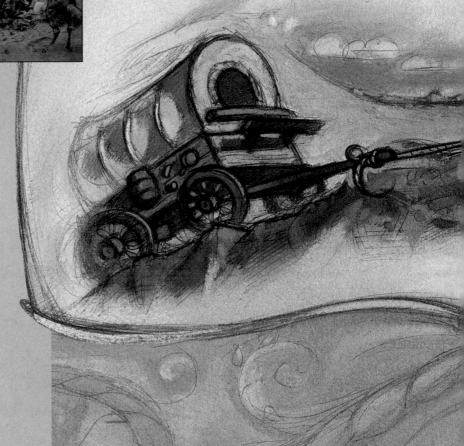

A Cowboy's Rope

by Tod Cody

The braided rawhide leather rope the *vaquero* used was called *la reata,* and this was changed by the cowboy into "lariat." The lariat's main use was for lassoing, but it was also used to drag firewood, to haul out wagons stuck in the mud, and to build makeshift corrals.

Roping was the most difficult thing a cowboy had to learn, but every cowboy had to be skilled with his lariat so that he could go about his daily business. A lariat could be anywhere between 30 and 60 ft (9 and 18 m) long, depending on the job for which it was needed.

LOOK AHEAD

In *Anthony Reynoso: Born to Rope*, a boy has a special skill with a cowboy's rope. Read to find out what the author's purpose is for writing about Anthony.

Vocabulary

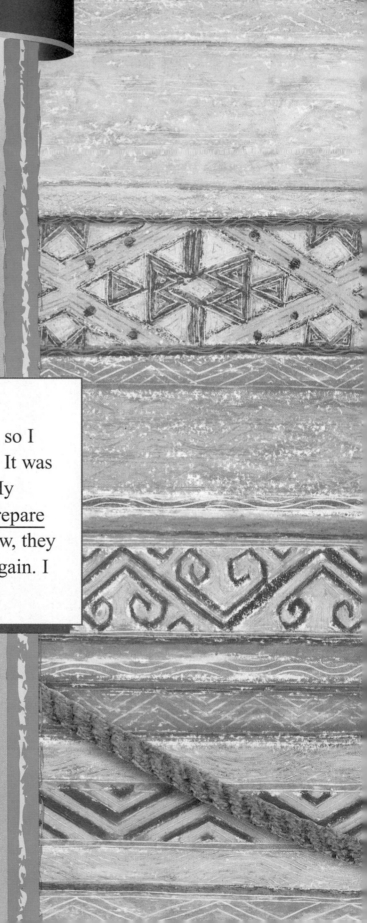

Words to Know

favorite	practice	tourists
rodeo	prepare	grandfather

When you read, you may come across words you don't know. Look for clues in the words or sentences near the word to figure out what it means.

Read this paragraph. Figure out the meaning of *practice* by reading the words around it.

Ride 'Em Cowboy!

I was curious about what a <u>rodeo</u> is like, so I asked my <u>grandfather</u> to take me to one. It was fun being <u>tourists</u> with other travelers. My <u>favorite</u> part was watching the clowns <u>prepare</u> and <u>practice</u> for their act. Before the show, they do funny and hard stunts over and over again. I hope I can be in a rodeo someday.

Write About It

Where would you like to travel?
Write a postcard from your trip.
Use some of the vocabulary words.

ANTHONY REYNOSO
Born to Rope

**BY MARTHA COOPER
AND GINGER GORDON**

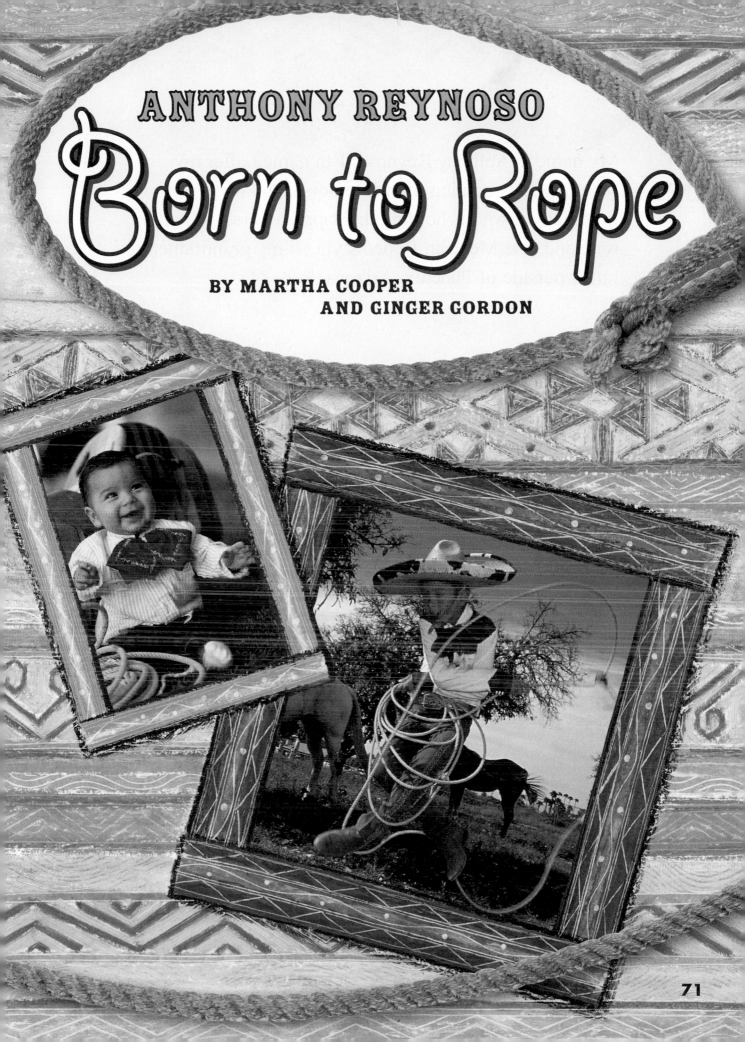

My name is Anthony Reynoso. I'm named after my father, who is holding the white horse, and my grandfather, who is holding the dappled horse. We all rope and ride Mexican Rodeo style on my grandfather's ranch outside of Phoenix, Arizona.

As soon as I could stand, my dad gave me a rope. I had my own little hat and everything else I needed to dress as a *charro*. That's what a Mexican cowboy is called.

It's a good thing I started when I was little, because it takes years to learn to rope.

I live with my mom and dad in the little Mexican American and Yaqui Indian town of Guadalupe. All my grandparents live close by. This will help a lot when the new baby comes. My mom is pregnant.

I've got a secret about Guadalupe. I know where there are petroglyphs in the rocks right near my house. My favorite looks like a man with a shield. People carved these petroglyphs hundreds of years ago. Why did they do it? I wonder what the carvings mean.

Every Sunday morning the old Mexican Mission church is packed. At Easter, lots of people come to watch the Yaqui Indian ceremonies in the center of town. No one's allowed to take photographs, but an artist painted a wall showing the Yaqui dancers.

MENUDO &
FOOD SALE
SUN. 7ᴬᴹ-12ᴾᴹ
YAQUI
HALL

Some Sundays, we go to Casa Reynoso, my grandparents' restaurant. If it's very busy, my cousins and I pitch in. When there's time, my grandmother lets me help in the kitchen. Casa Reynoso has the best Mexican food in town.

On holidays, we go to my grandfather's ranch. Once a year, we all get dressed up for a family photo.

I've got lots of cousins. Whenever there's a birthday we have a piñata. We smash it with a stick until all the candy falls out. Then we scramble to grab as much as we can hold.

Best of all, at the ranch we get to practice roping on horseback. My dad's always trying something new . . . and so am I!

In Mexico, the Rodeo is the national sport. The most famous charros there are like sports stars here.

On weekdays, Dad runs his landscape business, Mom works in a public school, and I go to school. I wait for the bus with other kids at the corner of my block.

I always come to school with my homework done. When I'm in class, I forget about roping and riding. I don't think anyone in school knows about it except my best friends.

It's different when I get home. I practice hard with Dad. He's a good teacher and shows me everything his father taught him. We spend a lot of time practicing for shows at schools, malls, and rodeos. We are experts at passing the rope. Our next big exhibition is in Sedona, about two hours away by car.

After rope practice we shoot a few baskets. Dad's pretty good at that too!

On Friday after school, Dad and I prepare our ropes for the show in Sedona. They've got to be just right.

Everything's ready for tomorrow, so I can take a break and go through my basketball cards. I decide which ones I want to buy, sell, and trade. Collecting basketball cards is one of my favorite hobbies.

It's Saturday! Time for the show in Sedona. I get a little nervous watching the other performers. I sure wouldn't want to get messed up in my own rope in front of all these people!

After the Mexican hat dance, we're next!

My dad goes first . . .

and then it's my turn. While the mariachis play, I do my stuff.

Even Dad can't spin the rope from his teeth like this!

Then Dad and I rope together, just like we practiced. It's hard to do with our wide charro hats on. When my dad passes the rope to me and I spin it well, he says he has passed the Mexican Rodeo tradition on to me. Now it's up to me to keep it going.

Mom is our best fan. She always comes with us. It makes me feel good to know she's out there watching.

Sometimes tourists want us to pose for pictures with them. It makes me feel like a celebrity.

After the show, boy, are we hungry! We pack up and eat a quick lunch. Then we go to a special place called Slide Rock.

Slide Rock is a natural water slide where kids have played for hundreds, maybe even thousands, of years. It's cold today! I'd rather come back in the summer when it's hot. But Dad pulls me in anyway. Brrr!

Time to go home. Next time we come to Sedona, the baby will be with us. I wonder if it will be a boy or a girl. It's hard to wait!

I'm going to love being a big brother. Pretty soon the baby will be wearing my old boots and learning how to rope from me.

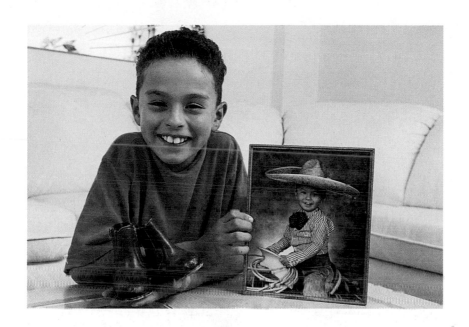

About the Photographer and the Author

MARTHA COOPER
GINGER GORDON

Anthony Reynoso: Born to Rope is a true story told in photographs about a Mexican American boy.

Martha Cooper took the pictures of Anthony Reynoso and his family. She has taken pictures for other books and magazines too.

Ginger Gordon, a teacher in New York City, wrote the words to go along with the pictures. She says she gets her ideas from her students.

Reader Response

Open for Discussion

Roping takes a lot of practice. Do you think everyone could learn to rope? Why or why not?

Comprehension Check

1. Do you think Anthony enjoys roping? Find parts of the story to explain why you think as you do.

2. Look back on pages 80 and 81. Name other things Anthony does besides roping.

3. In *How I Spent My Summer Vacation,* Wallace also learns to rope and do tricks. Who do you think would be better at roping and doing tricks, Anthony or Wallace? Use details from each story to explain your answer.

4. **Author's purpose** is the writer's reason for writing. Name one important purpose the author had for writing about Anthony. Why do you think so? (Author's Purpose)

5. Often an **author** has more than one **purpose** for writing. Name another reason the author had for writing about Anthony. Why do you think so? (Author's Purpose)

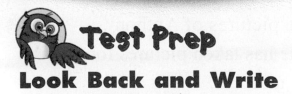

Test Prep

Look Back and Write

Anthony Reynoso's family is very important to him. Look back at pages 76–78 and pages 83–85. Use details to explain what Anthony's family means to him.

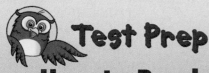

1. Preview

- A picture essay shows a main idea and details through pictures and words. Find these features in the picture essay on pages 87–89:

    caption–words near a picture that tell what it is

    label–a name for a picture

    callout–information connected to a picture by a line

2. Read and Locate Information

- Read the picture essay. Go back and point out parts that remind you of what you read in *Anthony Reynoso.*

3. Think and Connect

Think about *Anthony Reynoso* and the information you found in "People and Horses."

What information from "People and Horses" would you add to *Anthony Reynoso*? Why?

People AND Horses

by David H. Murdoch

People and horses have worked together since wild horses were first tamed—about 5,000 years ago. Since then, horses have changed human history. They have allowed nomads, or traveling peoples, to spread across continents. They have transported soldiers in war. They have been important to farmers and cattle ranchers.

The Spanish settlers of Mexico brought horses and cattle to the Americas, which had none until then. Some horses escaped into the wild to become the mustangs of the U.S., the *pasos* of Peru, and the *criollos* of Argentina.

THE GAUCHOS' COW PONY
Like the mustang of the north, the *criollo,* or cow pony, came from horses that wandered into South America from Mexico.

EYEWITNESS

The Best Horses

There are few wild horses left, but all present-day horses come from them. Farmers and ranchers have crossed one kind of horse with another. Also, horses have been raised in different environments. As a result, there are now horses of different colors, sizes, abilities, and characteristics.

TURN HIM LOOSE, BILL
This painting by Frederic Remington shows a cowboy "breaking" an untamed horse.

Built-in saddlebag

MONGOL PONY
About a thousand years ago, Genghis Khan and his conquering army rode shaggy Mongol ponies. Herdsmen in northwest China still ride these kinds of horses.

TEXAS COW PONY
This Texas cowboy is riding a mustang. Both Native Americans and cowboys used mustangs. Though small, the cow pony was hard working.

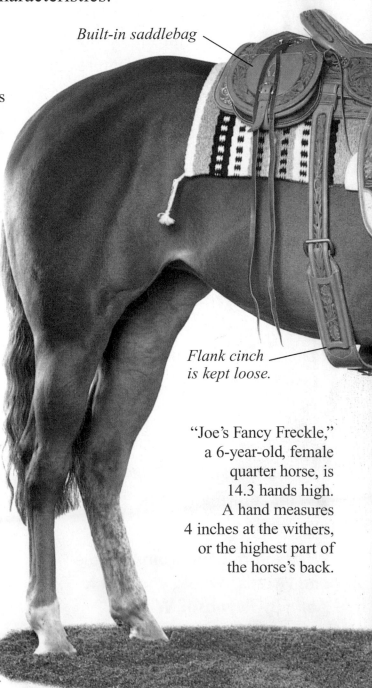

Flank cinch is kept loose.

"Joe's Fancy Freckle," a 6-year-old, female quarter horse, is 14.3 hands high. A hand measures 4 inches at the withers, or the highest part of the horse's back.

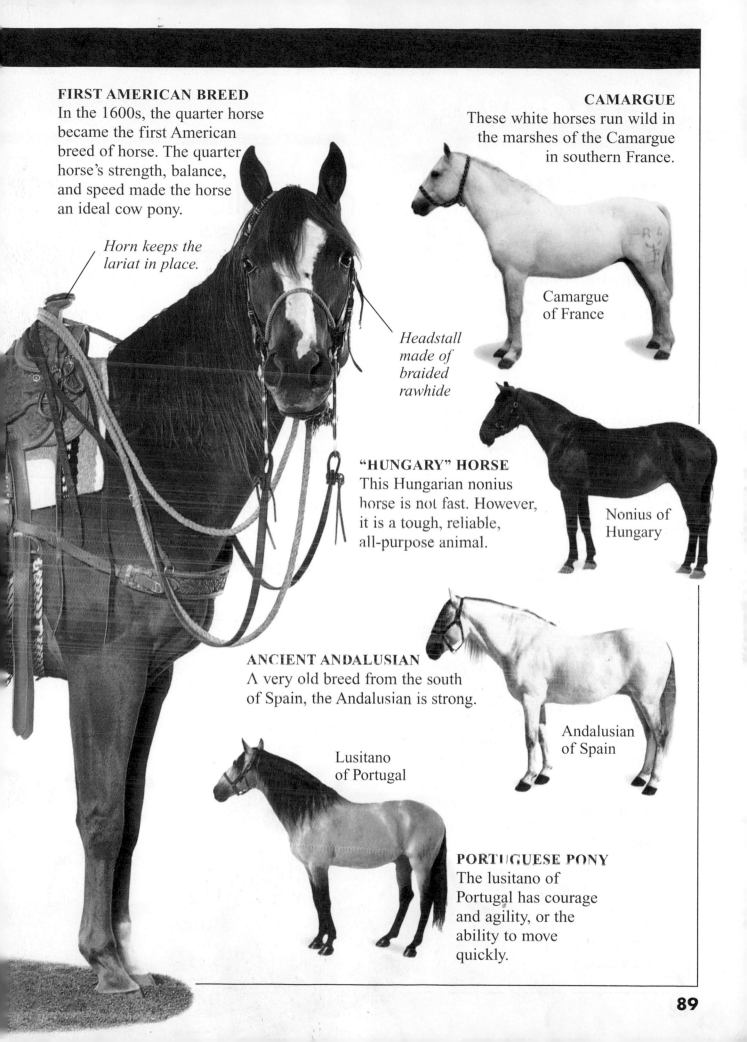

FIRST AMERICAN BREED
In the 1600s, the quarter horse became the first American breed of horse. The quarter horse's strength, balance, and speed made the horse an ideal cow pony.

Horn keeps the lariat in place.

Headstall made of braided rawhide

CAMARGUE
These white horses run wild in the marshes of the Camargue in southern France.

Camargue of France

"HUNGARY" HORSE
This Hungarian nonius horse is not fast. However, it is a tough, reliable, all-purpose animal.

Nonius of Hungary

ANCIENT ANDALUSIAN
A very old breed from the south of Spain, the Andalusian is strong.

Lusitano of Portugal

Andalusian of Spain

PORTUGUESE PONY
The lusitano of Portugal has courage and agility, or the ability to move quickly.

Cause and Effect

- A **cause** is why something happens.

- An **effect** is what happens.

- Clue words can sometimes signal causes and effects.

- As you read, look for clue words, such as *if, then, because, since,* and *so,* to help you understand what happens and why it happens.

Read "Annabelle's Party" from *Herbie Jones* by Suzy Kline.

Write About It

1. Write the words *cause* and *effect* at the top of a sheet of paper. List some things that happen under *effect* and why they happen under *cause.*

2. Write down some clue words that signal what happens and why.

Annabelle's Party
by Suzy Kline

The phone rang, so Herbie picked it up. "Hello?"

"Double 030?"

Herbie cupped the phone and whispered, "Yeah . . . just a minute, 992." Herbie moved the phone and phone cord through the dining room and into the pantry off the kitchen. When he closed the door a rack of onions fell on him.

"What's that?" Raymond asked.

"Nothing, 992, just a bunch of onions."

"Huh?"

"Never mind. What's so important that we have to use code language?"

"You're getting an invitation to Annabelle Louisa Hodgekiss's birthday party."

Herbie sat down on two onions. "You've got to be kidding."

"Nope. I was at Mr. D's store and I heard Annabelle tell her mother that she needed nine invitations this year because she wanted to invite you to her birthday."

"Where were you?"

"Behind the magic markers. I wanted to find a purple one. Her mother was mad, too, because she had to buy another package of invitations. They only came eight to a package."

"Man, why do you suppose she wants ME to come?"

"Well, you're the spelling champ and all."

Herbie picked up the two onions he had been sitting on and started juggling them in the air. "I wish people would forget about that. Now I feel like I have to get a hundred every Friday—especially when Dad asks to see my spelling test as soon as I get home."

"That's deadly. Hey Herbie, I was thinkin', do you suppose Annabelle might use a few of those extra invitations?"

"Maybe."

"If she does, I bet she invites me too. She knows I'm your best friend."

LOOK AHEAD

In "Herbie and Annabelle," Herbie continues to have adventures with his classmates. Read and find out what happens and why.

Vocabulary

Words to Know

coughs   pretend   discovered
secret   poems   sheet
curious

Many words have more than one meaning. To decide what a word means, look for clues in the words around it.

Read the list. Decide if *sheet* means "a piece of cloth" or "a single piece of paper."

Things to Do When Sick

When Joe <u>coughs</u> and stays in bed, he makes a list of things to do.
1. Find out who <u>discovered</u> the planets.
2. Write some silly <u>poems</u>.
3. <u>Pretend</u> to be famous and on TV.
4. Make up a <u>secret</u> code.
5. Read a book under the <u>sheet</u>.
6. Make up a story about a <u>curious</u> dog.

Write About It

Use vocabulary words to write a sick friend a get well card.

Herbie
and
Annabelle

by Suzy Kline

Who's Who

Herbie Jones likes to read but he has been in the lowest reading group for most of his life. He carries a notebook, writes poems, reads books about spiders, and enjoys teasing his older sister, Olivia. He hates doing skill sheets in his third-grade class at Laurel Woods Elementary School. Sometimes he uses his spy code number—Double 030—when he talks to his best friend, Raymond Martin, on the phone. Herbie cares what his parents think.

Annabelle Louisa Hodgekiss is the smartest girl in third grade. She is bossy and can be mean, but she works hard, is very neat, and always obeys the rules. When she's angry with Herbie, she gives him the silent treatment or puts red checks after his name in her notepad. She's a good athlete and tries to be first in every contest. Her initials, ALH, are on most of her things.

Mr. Hodgekiss is Annabelle's father. He likes making eggplant parmigiana, watching Annabelle play baseball, and cracking jokes. Annabelle doesn't think they're funny. Herbie does.

Narrator is like a stage manager. He or she establishes the setting, time, and character motivation. When necessary, this person moves the action.

SFX Person is the Sound Effects Person who makes special noises.

Characters: Narrator
  SFX Person
  Herbie Jones
  Mr. Hodgekiss
  Annabelle Louisa Hodgekiss
Setting: Annabelle's house
Time: After school

NARRATOR: Herbie rang Annabelle's doorbell.

SFX PERSON: Bzzzzzzz. Bzzzzzz.

HERBIE: I wish I didn't have to deliver these get well cards from the class. But the teacher said I *had* to because I live the closest. *(groans)*

NARRATOR: Mr. Hodgekiss answered the door.

MR. HODGEKISS: Hello, Herbie.

HERBIE: Hello, Mr. Hodgekiss. My teacher wanted me to drop these cards by for Annabelle. Would you please give them to her? *(waves good-bye)* Thanks, bye.

NARRATOR: Herbie turned around and headed down the steps.

MR. HODGEKISS: Just a minute, Herbie. Won't you come in and give the cards to Annabelle yourself? The doctor said she isn't contagious anymore.

HERBIE: *(to himself)* Whoa. I was supposed to deliver these cards to the door. Not go *in*. Miss Pinkham never said I had to do *that*.

MR. HODGEKISS: Just for a minute?

SFX PERSON: *(clears throat)*

HERBIE: Well . . . okay, Mr. Hodgekiss.

NARRATOR: Herbie felt his throat getting dry and raspy as he walked inside the house. When they got to Annabelle's door, they stopped.

MR. HODGEKISS: Before we go in, I must tell you something. Annabelle has been very stubborn about having the chicken pox.

SFX PERSON: *(clears throat again)*

HERBIE: *(answers like a squeaky frog)* Reaaaally?

NARRATOR: Herbie tried to act surprised but the fact was Herbie already knew Annabelle was stubborn—about everything.

MR. HODGEKISS: She insists on putting the sheet over her head every time someone comes in the room. She won't even let *me* see her face. Just her mother. She says when the spots and scabs are gone in a few days, she won't hide behind the sheet.

HERBIE: *(to Mr. Hodgekiss)* No kidding? Annabelle has a sheet over her head? *(to himself)* This is great! I didn't want to see her anyway.

MR. HODGEKISS: Maybe you'll have better luck. *(knocks on door)* May we come in, Annabelle?

ANNABELLE: Who's with you?

MR. HODGEKISS: Someone from school. He has some get well cards for you.

NARRATOR: Mr. Hodgekiss opened the door slowly. Herbie saw Annabelle sitting up in bed. The sheet was tucked behind her head.

ANNABELLE: Who is it?

MR. HODGEKISS: See for yourself, dear.

NARRATOR: Mr. Hodgekiss smiled as he walked out of the room. Herbie quickly looked around and sat down in a chair by Annabelle's desk.

SFX PERSON: *(coughs a few times and then clears throat)*

HERBIE: Hi . . . hi . . . Annabelle.

ANNABELLE: Do you have a cold, John, or is that your asthma acting up again?

HERBIE: *(to himself)* John? Hey, this could be fun. I'm visiting a ghost and now I can even pretend to be someone else. *(to Annabelle)* Just . . . just my asthma.

ANNABELLE: Did you bring me some cards?

HERBIE: Yup. Here's two.

ANNABELLE: Read them to me.

HERBIE: Sure. Here's one with a Viking ship on it.

ANNABELLE: I know that's from Raymond Martin. He always draws Viking ships.

HERBIE: Yup, and on the inside it says, "Bon Voyage."

ANNABELLE: BON VOYAGE? That's dumb. Bon Voyage means have a good trip. Having the chicken pox is NOT having fun, and you certainly can't go anywhere.

NARRATOR: Herbie remembered to cough a few times and act like John.

SFX PERSON: *(coughs, wheezes, and sneezes)*

HERBIE: Here's a real nice card. It has you in bed with your cat and a thermometer in your mouth.

ANNABELLE: Hmmmmm. I wonder who made that one?

HERBIE: It even has a poem inside. I'll read it.

Annabelle, Annabelle,
Sick in bed,
Spots on her nose
And spots on her head.
Think I will give her a
Bright red rose.
Then she knows
I will tickle her toes
With it.

ANNABELLE: *(giggles)* That's funny! Who wrote it?

NARRATOR: Herbie tipped back his chair.

HERBIE: Herbie Jones.

ANNABELLE: Herbie Jones wrote *that?*

HERBIE: The one and only.

NARRATOR: Annabelle was quiet for a moment.

ANNABELLE: Well, you know, John . . .

HERBIE: Yes, Annabelle . . .

ANNABELLE: I'm not speaking to Herbie . . .

HERBIE: Oh?

NARRATOR: Herbie leaned forward and listened. He was curious why Annabelle had put three red checks after his name on her notepad at school.

ANNABELLE: Herbie Jones wore earrings to school in October. It was Halloween, and he was supposed to be a pirate. Everyone knows a pirate wears just one *gold* earring. Herbie wore a pair of strawberries.

HERBIE: *(to himself)* That's check one.

ANNABELLE: . . . and when he wrote a story at Thanksgiving about a turkey who got his head chopped off, he called the turkey Annabelle.

HERBIE: *(Trying not to laugh, he holds up two fingers for victory.)*

ANNABELLE: *(groans)* . . . *and* he gave me a can of *salmon* for my birthday.

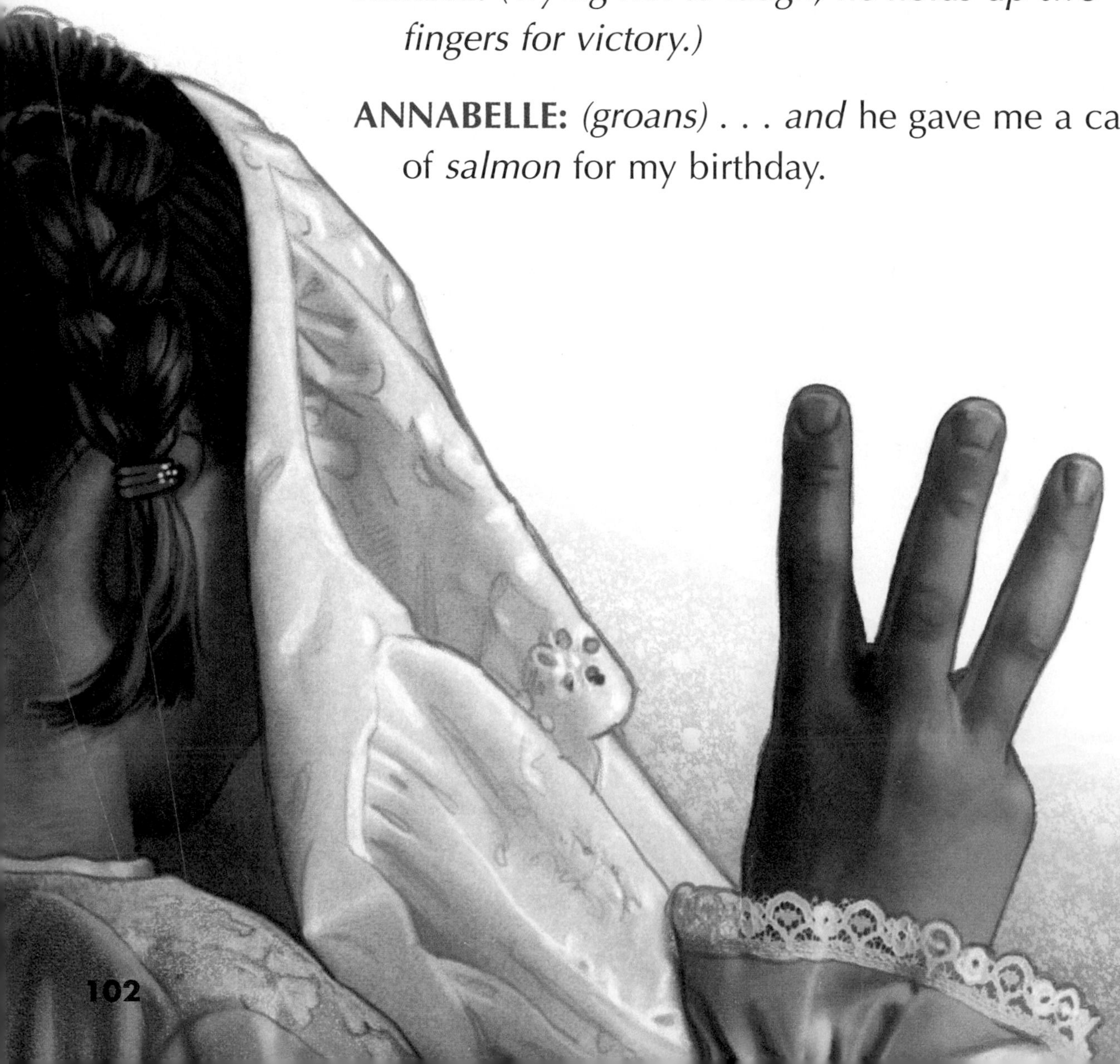

HERBIE: *(to himself)* Check three. What a memory she has. I better get out of here. It's getting dangerous. I've played John long enough. I'll sneeze once and then head for the door.

SFX PERSON: *(sneezes once loudly)*

ANNABELLE: But . . . Herbie Jones does have a way with words.

NARRATOR: Herbie stopped at the door.

HERBIE: Herbie Jones has a way with words?

ANNABELLE: IF YOU TELL HERBIE I SAID THAT, JOHN GREENWEED, I'LL HATE YOU FOREVER!

NARRATOR: Herbie snatched a Kleenex from the flowered box on Annabelle's desk and held it up to his mouth. This was no time to be discovered.

HERBIE: I won't. Your secret is safe with me. *(removes Kleenex and smiles)*

NARRATOR: Mr. Hodgekiss saw Herbie to the door.

MR. HODGEKISS: Did she talk to you face to face?

HERBIE: *(feeling guilty)* No. She even thinks . . . I'm . . . John Greenweed. I kind of went along with it.

MR. HODGEKISS: Listen, Herbie, if my daughter wants to play games, you can too. Your secret is safe with me . . . John.

HERBIE: Thanks, Mr. Hodgekiss!

NARRATOR: As Herbie shuffled along the sidewalk, he kept thinking about what Annabelle had said. Herbie Jones has a way with words.

HERBIE: Is that really true? Maybe I should try making up a few more poems. Let's see . . .

Spaghetti is red.
Meatballs are brown.
You make them with eggs
And a pound of ground round.

When the sun is yellow,
It's time to play.
When the sun is red,
It's time to go to bed.

(clicks fingers) I do have a way with words!

About the Author

Suzy Kline

When she is not teaching
her own students, Suzy Kline
likes to talk to other students
about what it is like to be a writer.
She points out that not everything she has written
has been accepted by publishers. "I always bring
my bag of rejections," she says. This lets children
know that "the first book I got published was not
the first book I wrote." She also likes to show
things that have given her ideas for stories—
such as green slime and light-bulb necklaces.

Since she is busy teaching during most of the
day, Ms. Kline does a lot of her writing early in
the morning. She even writes in the bathtub!

Ms. Kline has written many award-winning
stories about Herbie and Annabelle, the characters
in this story. She knows them so well that she
considers them almost part of her family.

Reader Response

Open for Discussion

Would you like classmates to visit if you were home sick? Why or why not?

Comprehension Check

1. Look back on page 97. Do you think Annabelle is ashamed of the way she looks with chicken pox? Use details to explain.

2. Look back on pages 95–97. Herbie doesn't want to go into Annabelle's house. What are some things he says and does that give you clues?

3. This story is told like a play. Do you think it is easier or harder to read this way? Use details from the story to explain your answer.

4. A **cause** is why something happens. An **effect** is what happens. Why doesn't Annabelle know that Herbie is pretending to be John? (Cause and Effect)

5. Herbie makes up a poem after leaving Annabelle's house. What **caused** him to do that? (Cause and Effect)

 Test Prep

Look Back and Write

Look back on page 98. Annabelle thinks Herbie is John. Why do you think Herbie doesn't tell her who he is? Use details from the story to explain your answer.

What Are Viruses?

by Leslie Jean LeMaster

Viruses are one-celled germs that are much smaller than bacteria. They only can be seen under very powerful microscopes.

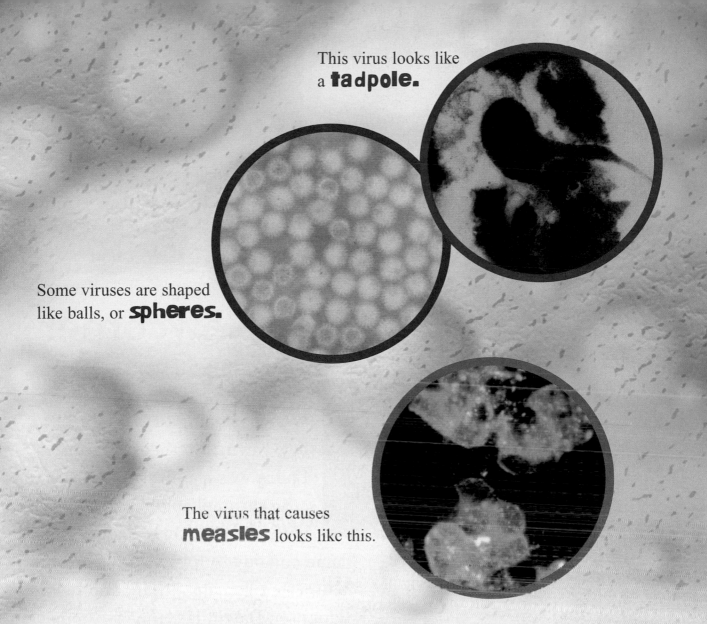

This virus looks like a **tadpole.**

Some viruses are shaped like balls, or **spheres.**

The virus that causes **measles** looks like this.

Some viruses are shaped like spheres. Some are rod-shaped and have many sides. Some look like tadpoles. They can grow and multiply only in living cells. Many viruses are not harmful. If enough harmful viruses get inside your body cells and grow, you get sick.

Like bacteria, viruses can cause many diseases. Some viruses cause diseases of the skin, such as chicken pox and measles. Others cause diseases of nerve tissue, such as rabies and polio. And still other viruses cause diseases of body organs, such as the flu and the common cold.

Few medicines can kill viruses. Usually your body's own germ killers will kill viruses over a period of time.

Skill Lesson

Character

- A **character** is a person or animal in a story.

- Authors tell us about characters when they describe what characters say, do, and feel.

Read "The Newcomer" from *Because You're Lucky* by Irene Smalls.

Talk About It

1. What actions tell you how Dawn feels about Kevin?

2. What clues give you some idea about the kind of character Dawn's mother is?

The Newcomer
by Irene Smalls

Who was going to take Hazel's boy, Kevin? Softhearted Aunt Laura was the first to say yes.

So caramel-colored Kevin with the long curly lashes came one day to live with his aunt Laura, her son, Jonathan, and her daughter, Dawn. He came without a toothbrush or a toy. He came without a change of clothes, and he came without a mommy or a daddy.

Tall teenaged Dawn answered the door.

She eyed the tiny newcomer suspiciously. "Momma, how come that raggedy little boy has to come

ittle allowed

live with us?" she complained to her mother after she had let him in.

"Because I'm his aunt and you and Jonathan are his cousins and he's family. Family has to stick together," her mother answered firmly.

"Hello, Cousin Kevin. How very nice it is to meet you. We're delighted to have you come to stay with us," Jonathan's mother said loudly to Kevin.

"Hmmph," Dawn sniffed. She brushed past Kevin and went into her room, closing the door behind her. A few minutes later, the door reopened. Dawn reached out and hung a sign on it: NO LITTLE BOYS ALLOWED.

LOOK AHEAD

In *Allie's Basketball Dream,* Allie wants to do well at playing basketball. Read and discover what kind of character she is.

Vocabulary

Words to Know

aimed	gift	basketball
bounced	shoot	playground

Words with similar meanings, such as *big* and *large,* are **synonyms.** You can often figure out the meaning of an unknown word by finding a clue in the words around it. Sometimes this clue is a synonym.

Read this paragraph. Notice how *present* helps you understand what *gift* means.

The Winning Shot

Morgan <u>bounced</u> the <u>basketball</u> down the court. Could she <u>shoot</u> the winning basket? She <u>aimed</u>, threw the ball, watched it soar through the air, and cheered when it went in! She helped her team win the <u>playground</u> contest. Her parents gave her a special present. The <u>gift</u> was a ticket to a professional basketball game.

Talk About It

Imagine you are a sportscaster at a professional game. Tell what you see. Use vocabulary words.

by Barbara E. Barber • illustrated by Darryl Ligasan

ALLIE'S
BASKETBALL DREAM

When Allie's father came home from work Friday evening, he brought her a gift. "Because I love you," he said, and kissed Allie on her nose. The gift was something that Allie really wanted—a basketball.

The next day, Allie and her father walked to the playground. Allie loved the sound her new basketball made as she bounced it on the sidewalk. As they passed the firehouse, they waved to Mr. Puchinsky, the fire captain.

"Hi, Domino!" Allie called to the firehouse dog. Domino wagged his tail and licked Allie's basketball when she held it for him to sniff.

At the playground, Allie scanned the basketball courts while her father talked with Mr. Gonzalez, the park monitor. Some older kids already had a game going. All of the players were boys. They hardly ever missed a shot.

"Go ahead and practice, and then we'll shoot baskets together as soon as I get back from taking Aunt Harriet shopping," Allie's father told her. "I'll just be across the street. If you need me, tell Mr. Gonzalez, and he'll come get me."

"Okay," Allie replied.

She waved good-bye and ran to an empty court. She lifted her new basketball over her head and aimed. The shot missed. She aimed again. She missed again.

One of the boys playing in the next court noticed Allie and started to laugh. The others joined in.

"*Boys*," Allie mumbled. Then she dribbled and bounced. And bounced and dribbled.

Allie's friend Keisha came into the playground with her hula hoop. Keisha saw Allie and held the hoop up. Allie aimed her basketball and . . . *Zoom!* Right through the middle.

"Let's play basketball!" Allie said.

"I don't know how," Keisha answered.

"I'll show you."

Keisha twirled her hula hoop. "My brother says basketball's a boy's game."

"Your brother doesn't know what he's talking about," Allie said.

She aimed at an empty trash can. She stepped back a few feet, and took a shot.

Thump! In!

Allie noticed her neighbor Buddy jumping rope with her friend Sheba and another girl. When he missed he ran off to join some other kids who wanted to use his volleyball.

"Hi, Allie!" Sheba called. "Is that your basketball?"

"Yep, my dad gave it to me. Want to shoot some baskets?"

"Maybe later," Sheba replied. "Want to jump double-dutch?"

"Maybe later," Allie said.

Allie pretended she was playing soccer. She kicked the ball and chased it. Then she looked up at the basket, aimed, and shot. The ball struck the backboard, then the rim, and bounded off.

Julio, who was in Allie's class at school, whizzed by on his skateboard. He made a sharp turn when he noticed the new basketball.

"Wow!" Julio exclaimed. "Is that yours?"

"Yes," said Allie proudly. "Let's shoot some baskets!"

Julio looked at Allie, his eyes wide. "You must be kidding!" he said. "Me shoot baskets with a girl? No thanks!" He laughed and skated away.

Allie heaved a sigh and eyed the basket. She took another shot. The ball circled the rim and fell off. She heard some of the boys in the next court chuckle. She tried again. And again.

Allie sighed again and plopped down on a bench. Buddy walked over, bouncing his volleyball. "What's up?" he asked. "Something wrong with your basketball?"

"Well . . ." Allie hesitated.

"I'll trade you my volleyball for it! It's smaller and lighter—it'll be easier for you to play with."

"I don't know," Allie said.

Buddy reached into his pocket. He took out a miniature sports car, two quarters, and some grape bubble gum—Allie's favorite. "You can have these *and* my volleyball for the basketball," he said.

Allie thought it over. She remembered the first time her father took her to a basketball game at Madison Square Garden. She loved it all: The noise of the crowd, the bright lights on the court, and especially the slam-dunks the players made look so easy! She knew right then and there that one day, she would be a professional basketball player too. . . .

Allie hugged her basketball close. "No way I'm getting rid of this ball! It's a gift from my dad. Someday I'm going to be the best basketball player ever!"

"Well," Buddy snorted, "some guys think girls shouldn't be playin' basketball."

"That's dumb!" Allie bounced her ball. "My cousin Gwen plays on one of the best high school teams in her state. She's won more than ten trophies!"

Buddy looked surprised.

"Some girls think boys shouldn't be jumping rope," Allie continued. "They think boys are no good at it. That's dumb too."

Buddy unwrapped two pieces of gum. "Want some?"

Allie and Buddy blew huge purple bubbles. They popped their gum so loud that Domino ran over to investigate. He pranced right up to Allie and sniffed her basketball.

"Wanna play basketball, Domino? Come on, boy, let's play!"

Domino ran alongside Allie as she dribbled and bounced. Laughing, Allie turned toward the basket, and took a long-distance shot. The ball brushed against the backboard, rolled around the rim, and dropped in!

Buddy jumped up from the bench. "Nice shot, Allie!" he yelled, and ran to retrieve the ball.

"Thanks," Allie said, beaming.

Julio saw the shot too. So did Sheba. They both hurried to the center of the court.

"Here!" Allie and Julio and Sheba called to Buddy almost in one voice.

Buddy dribbled the ball, then passed it to Allie. She took a shot and missed.

"Don't worry, Allie!" Buddy yelled. Julio and Sheba each shot and missed. Allie caught the ball and dribbled closer to the basket. *I can't wait to show Dad what I can do,* she thought.

Up, up went the ball. It didn't touch the backboard.
It didn't touch the rim. It didn't touch anything.

Zoom! In!

The older boys in the next court applauded. Mr.
Gonzalez whistled. Domino barked. Above all the noise
rose a familiar voice—Allie's father.

"That-a-girl!" he shouted. "Hooray for Allie!"

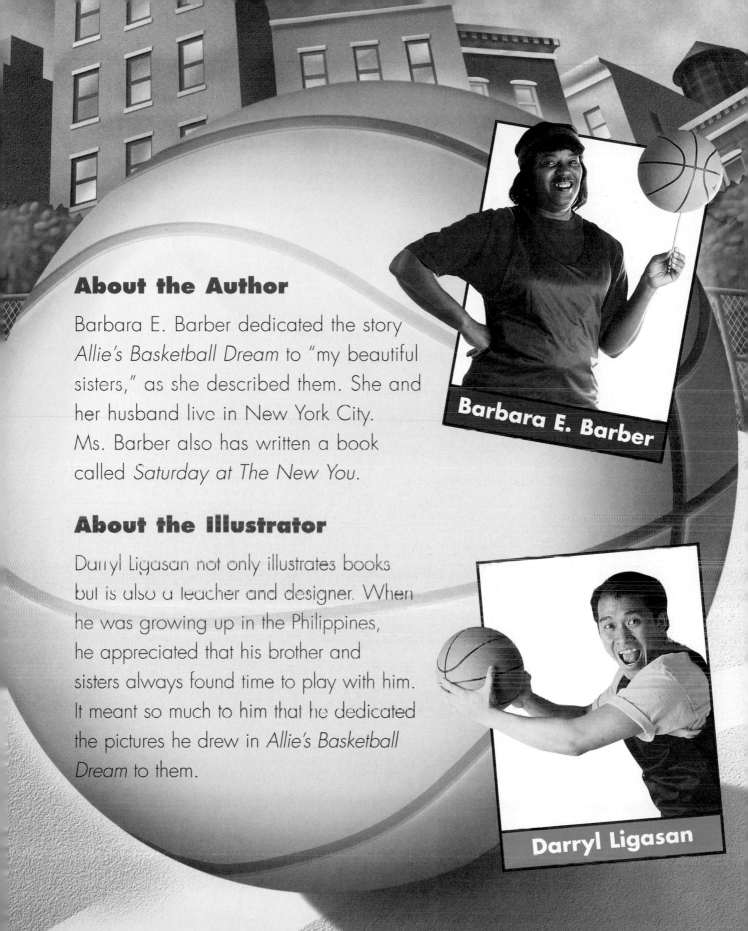

About the Author

Barbara E. Barber dedicated the story *Allie's Basketball Dream* to "my beautiful sisters," as she described them. She and her husband live in New York City. Ms. Barber also has written a book called *Saturday at The New You*.

Barbara E. Barber

About the Illustrator

Darryl Ligasan not only illustrates books but is also a teacher and designer. When he was growing up in the Philippines, he appreciated that his brother and sisters always found time to play with him. It meant so much to him that he dedicated the pictures he drew in *Allie's Basketball Dream* to them.

Darryl Ligasan

Reader Response

Open for Discussion

Pretend you are Allie's friend. What would you say or do to encourage her to keep trying?

Comprehension Check

1. Look back at page 115. How do you think Allie feels when her father gives her the basketball? Use details to explain.

2. Look back on pages 121–122. Why do you think Buddy wants Allie's basketball? Use details to explain.

3. On page 128 Allie hears her father's voice as she makes her final basket. Use details to explain why you think this might make her happy.

4. Allie is the main **character** in the story. She is determined. What actions or words in the story tell you what kind of person she is? (Character)

5. Allie dreams of playing professional basketball. You know what kind of **character** she is. Could she make her dream come true? Why or why not? (Character)

Test Prep
Look Back and Write

Look back at the pictures on pages 117–120. Explain how these pictures give clues to Allie's feelings. Use specific details to support your answer.

Test Prep

How to Read a Magazine Article

1. Preview

- This magazine article has four parts: an introduction and three photo features.

- Read the four titles. What kinds of tips will you find in each part?

2. Read and Make a List

- Read the article for tips on sinking foul shots. Write the best tip from each part.

Tips

1. Say to yourself, "The ball is going in!"
2.
3.
4.

3. Think and Connect

Think about *Allie's Basketball Dream.* Then look over your tips from "How to Sink Your Foul Shots."

Which tip on sinking foul shots would help Allie the most? Why?

How to Sink Your Foul Shots

written by Andrea N. Whittaker
photographed by Manny Millan

A foul shot is also called a free throw. Why? Because no one guards you when you shoot. Sinking a 15-foot free throw looks easy. But it takes a lot of work.

Carolyn Jones is a 5 foot 9 inch guard. She is an excellent foul shooter because she has proper technique, she concentrates, and she is confident.

"You have to be confident that you'll make the shot every time," says Carolyn. "You can't think, 'Oh, my gosh, what if I miss?!' Say to yourself, 'The ball is going in!' "

Here are some more of Carolyn's free throw tips.

Drills

Here are three drills to help you learn to release the ball properly.

Lying on Your Back

Shoot the ball so that it goes two or three feet straight up and straight back down. Snap your wrist as you release the ball.

Phone Booth

Imagine you are shooting up and out of a phone booth. Use one hand. This helps put the ball over the rim.

Chair Shot

When you shoot from a chair, you can't use your legs to help push the ball. Concentrate on your arms and wrists. Keep your shoulders facing the basket.

The Perfect Free Throw

If you are right-handed, stand with your right foot slightly forward. (Reverse the stance if you are left-handed.)

Get a feel for the basketball. I like to dribble three times before I shoot.

Hold the ball with your fingertips. Bend your shooting arm in an "L" shape. Place your nonshooting hand on the side of the ball to hold it in place.

Concentration

Great shooters love going to the line when the game is close and the crowd is going wild.

Focus on your shooting form. Tell yourself that the ball is going in!

Bend your knees a bit. Look at the entire basket, not just the front of the rim.

Lift the ball smoothly as you begin to straighten up. Tuck in the elbow of your shooting arm.

Extend your shooting arm. Snap your wrist. Don't jump. Release the ball when you're on your tiptoes.

My Brother Is as Generous as Anyone Could Be

by Jack Prelutsky

My brother is as generous
as anyone could be,
for everything he's ever had
he's always shared with me.
He has loaned me his binoculars,
his new computer games,
and his wind-up walking dragon
that breathes artificial flames.
I've been grateful for his robots,
for his giant teddy bear,
but not for certain other things
I'd hoped he'd never share—
Though I'm glad he's shared his rockets
and his magic jumping rocks,
I wish my brother hadn't shared
his case of chicken pox.

Summer Vacation

by Karama Fufuka

We read books in school
and we write stories
about what we did on
summer vacations.

This summer,
I played ball
and went to the beach
and Mama brought home
a brand-new baby.

135

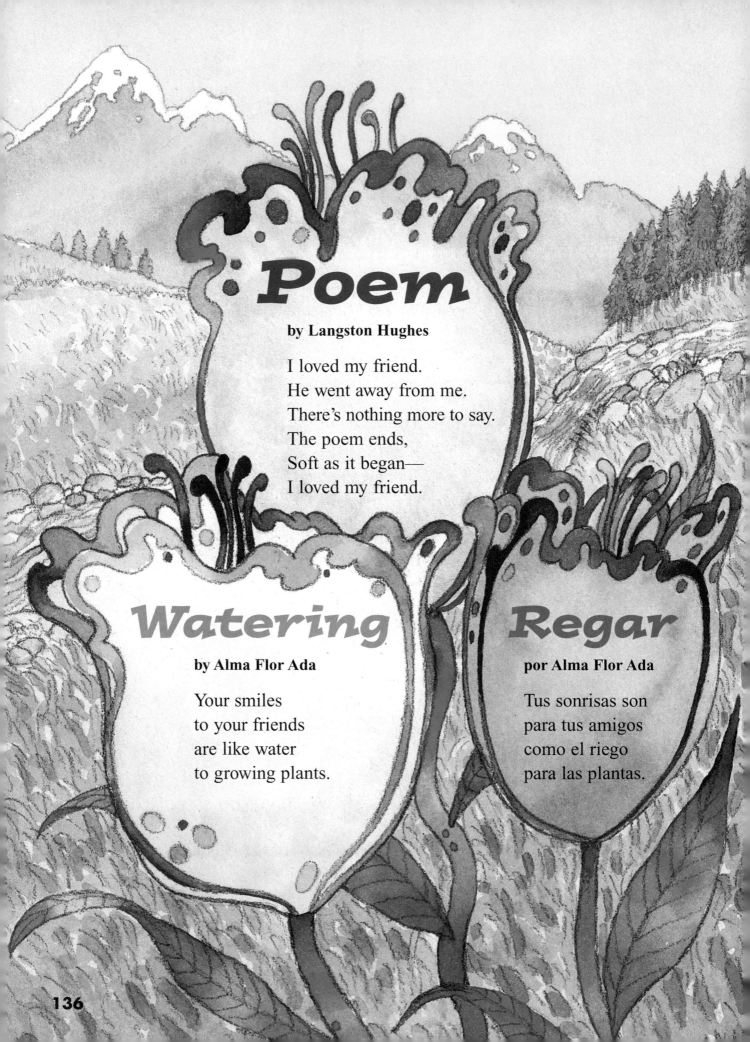

Poem

by Langston Hughes

I loved my friend.
He went away from me.
There's nothing more to say.
The poem ends,
Soft as it began—
I loved my friend.

Watering

by Alma Flor Ada

Your smiles
to your friends
are like water
to growing plants.

Regar

por Alma Flor Ada

Tus sonrisas son
para tus amigos
como el riego
para las plantas.

August afternoon

by Marion Edey

Where shall we go?
  What shall we play?
What shall we do
  On a hot summer day?

We'll sit in the swing.
  Go low. Go high.
And drink lemonade
  Till the glass is dry.

One straw for you,
  One straw for me,
In the cool green shade
  Of the walnut tree.

Wrap-Up

How do friends and family help us grow?

Calling All Actors

Perform a Scene

How do the characters and people you read about help each other to grow and learn?

1. **Reread** the selections and choose one scene that shows characters or people who grow and learn together.

2. **Decide** on the roles you and your classmates will perform. Practice the scene together.

3. **Present** your performance to the class.

Roving Reporter

Write a News Story

You work for a newspaper. Your job is to report on a surprising event.

1. **Choose** a surprising event from one selection.

2. **Focus** on what happens to the characters. Also think about when, where, why, and how.

3. **Write** your news story and then create an exciting headline for it.

Get Well Soon

Create a Get Well Card

Annabelle, in "Herbie and Annabelle", is your classmate. She is ill. Write a get well card to her.

1. **Think** about what you want to say to Annabelle.

2. **Fold** a sheet of paper in half and write your message inside.

3. **Draw** or **cut out** a picture to decorate the front of the card.

A Real Buckaroo

Show and Tell

Wallace, in *How I Spent My Summer Vacation*, couldn't wait for show and tell. It is now show and tell time. What do you think Wallace will bring?

1. **Decide** what Wallace will show his classmates. Will he show his wrangler outfit, a picture of the horse he rode, or a real steer?

2. **Plan** what you will show and what you will tell.

3. **Share** your show and tell with the class.

Test Talk

Understand the Question

Find Key Words in the Question

Before you can answer a test question, you have to understand it. A test about "How to Sink Your Foul Shots," pages 131–133, might have this question.

Test Question 1

How can you use your shooting arm to make the perfect free throw? Use details from the article to support your answer.

Read the question slowly.

Ask yourself "Who or what is this question about?" The words that tell who or what the question is about are **key words.**

Look for other key words in the question.

Often the first word of the question is a key word.

Turn the question into a statement.

Use the key words in a sentence that begins "I need to find out . . ."

See how one student makes sure she understands the question.

I've read the question. What is it about? Well, it's talking about my shooting arm and a perfect free throw. **Shooting arm** and **perfect free throw**— those must be key words.

Okay, I'm going to read the question again. There's the key word **how.** I need to find out how to use my shooting arm to make a perfect free throw.

Try it!

Now use what you learned to understand these test questions about "How to Sink Your Foul Shots," pages 131–133.

Test Question 2

What should you not do when you want to sink a foul shot? Find details from the article to support your answer.

Test Question 3

What should you say to yourself when you shoot a free throw?

Ⓐ "What if I miss?"

Ⓑ "The ball is going in!"

Ⓒ "I am going to miss!"

Ⓓ "I wonder who is watching me."

The Whole Wide World

How can we learn about and care for the world?

Graphic Sources

- A **graphic source** can be a picture, diagram, map, chart, graph, or something else that shows information.

- Graphic sources are useful because they show lots of information in an easy-to-see way.

- Making your own graphic, such as a chart, picture, or diagram, can help you understand what you read.

Read "Flowering Plants" from *What's Inside of Plants?* by Herbert S. Zim.

Talk About It

1. How does the diagram of the flowering plant help you understand the paragraph?

2. Look at the diagram. What parts of the plant shown do we usually eat?

FLOWERING PLANTS

by Herbert S. Zim

There are thousands of kinds of plants. Some are so small you can hardly see them. Other plants are the largest living things. The kinds of plants we see most often are the flowering plants. Peas, beans, corn, roses, and tomatoes are flowering plants. Most trees are flowering plants too. All flowering plants have leaves. They also have stems, roots, flowers, and fruits. Some are woody and grow for many years. Some grow one year and bloom the next. Some live and die in a single summer.

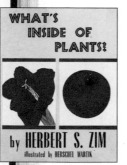

WHAT'S INSIDE OF PLANTS?

by HERBERT S. ZIM
illustrated by HERSCHEL WARTIK

Flower

Seed

Leaf

Fruit

Stem

Roots

Bean Plant

LOOK AHEAD

FLY TRAPS!
Plants That Bite Back

In *Fly Traps! Plants That Bite Back*, you will learn about plants that eat insects. Read and use the pictures to help you understand these plants.

Vocabulary

Words to Know

collect	pitcher	hinge
plants	insects	trap

When you read, you may come across a word you don't know. To figure out its meaning, look for clues around it. A clue might be found in the details or examples given near the unknown word.

Notice how *hinge* is used in the sentences below. Find details or examples in the same sentence. What do you think *hinge* means?

Surprising Plant

As I fill a <u>pitcher</u> with water to feed the <u>plants</u>, I notice <u>insects</u> crawling on the leaves of the Venus flytrap. The flytrap leaf has sticky hairs that feel an insect crawling. Then, just like a door with a <u>hinge</u>, the leaf closes down on the insect to <u>trap</u> it. I want to <u>collect</u> more of these interesting plants!

Talk About It

Would you want a Venus flytrap? Tell a friend why or why not. Use vocabulary words.

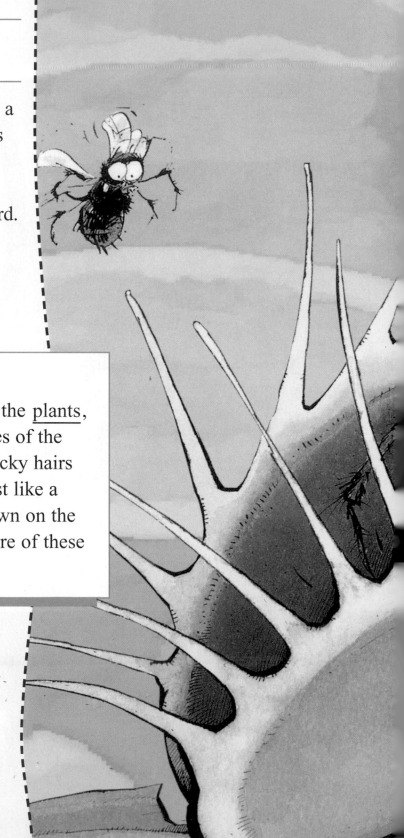

FLY TRAPS!

Plants That Bite Back

by Martin Jenkins / illustrated by David Parkins

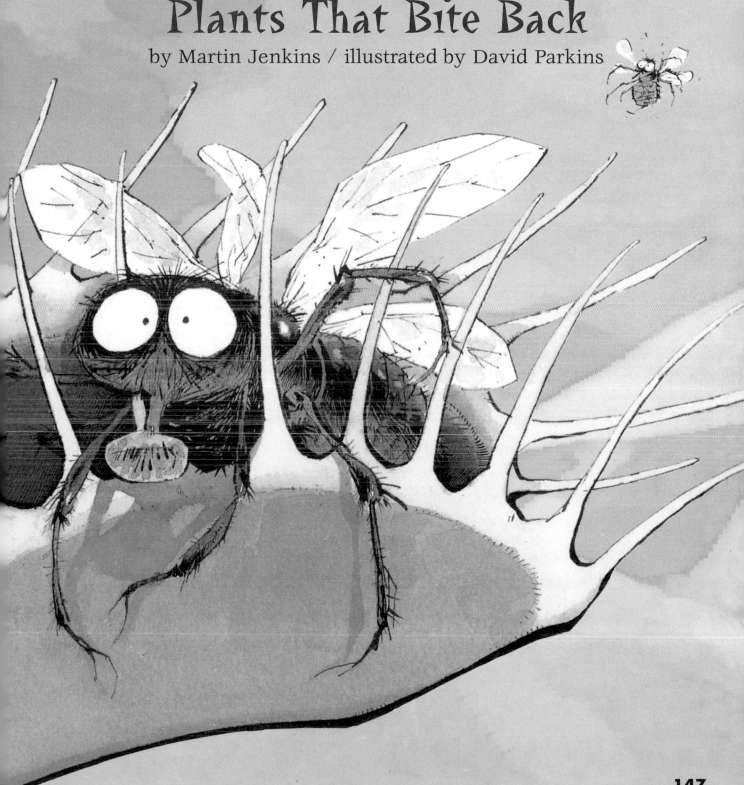

People do all sorts of things in their spare time. There are people who collect yogurt containers and people who make models out of bottle tops. There are beetle hunters and giant-leek growers.

Me, I like watching plants that eat animals.

Plants that eat animals are called carnivorous plants. There are hundreds of different kinds and they grow all around the world.

It all started with a plant I found in a pond. It had little yellow flowers sticking out of the water.

Under the water there were tangled stems with hundreds of tiny bubbles on them. A friend told me it was called a bladderwort.

There are over 200 different kinds of bladderworts. Most of them grow in ponds and rivers. They are usually very small, with narrow leaves and stems.

She said the bubbles on the stems were the bladders. Each one had a trap door shut tight, with little trigger hairs around it.

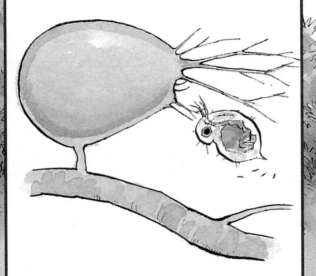

To set its traps, a bladderwort sucks the water out of its bladders.

Whenever a water flea or other bug touched a hair, the trap door swung back and in the bug went.

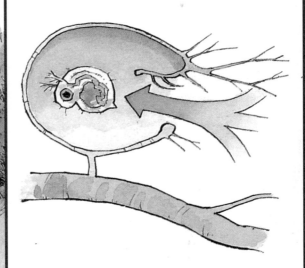

When a trap door opens, water rushes in, dragging the bug in with it.

Then the trap door slammed shut and there was no way out. And it all happened in the blink of an eye.

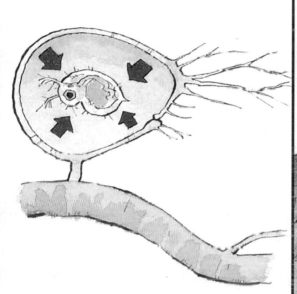

The bladderwort oozes special chemicals into the bladder. These dissolve the bug and the plant sucks it up.

Wow, that's neat, I thought. The trouble was, the traps on my plant were so small and so quick that I couldn't really see them work.

Well, I decided, I'll just have to find a bigger carnivorous plant.

So I did.

I had to climb a mountain, mind you, and walk through all its boggiest, mossiest places.

But there in the moss were little red plants, shining in the sun. I thought they were covered in dewdrops, but they weren't. They were sundews, and the shiny parts were sticky like honey. I'm sure you can guess what they were for.

When a bug gets stuck on a sundew, the leaf slowly curls up around it.

Then the soft parts of the bug are dissolved by chemicals and eaten.

I had to leave the sundews when the clouds rolled in. But as soon as I got home, I sent away for some sundew seeds of my own.

Afterward, the leaf opens up again and the leftover bug parts fall off.

Butterworts are carnivorous plants, too, and often grow in the same places as sundews. They have flat leaves like flypaper. Little bugs stick to the leaves and slowly dissolve.

The seeds weren't just for ordinary sundews, though. They were for Giant African sundews. I sowed them in a pot of moss and covered it with glass.

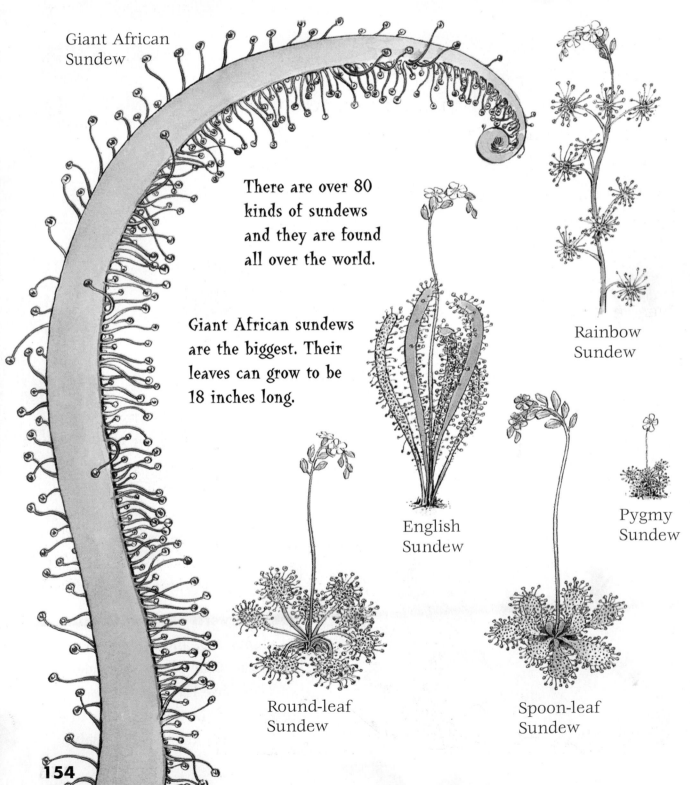

Giant African Sundew

There are over 80 kinds of sundews and they are found all over the world.

Giant African sundews are the biggest. Their leaves can grow to be 18 inches long.

Rainbow Sundew

English Sundew

Pygmy Sundew

Round-leaf Sundew

Spoon-leaf Sundew

I watered the pot every day with rainwater straight from the water tank. Soon the seeds started to sprout and I had dozens of baby sundews.

They grew and grew, until they were almost big enough to start catching things.

Then one day I watered them with the wrong kind of water—and every single one died.

I gave up on sundews after that, but I did grow a Venus flytrap. It lived on the windowsill and caught insects. Each of its leaves had a hinge down the center, several little trigger hairs, and a spiky rim.

When a fly or a wasp walked over a leaf, it was perfectly safe if it didn't touch any of the hairs. It was even safe if it touched just one of the hairs. But if it touched two of the hairs, then . . .

My sundews died because I accidentally put fertilizer in the water. All carnivorous plants hate fertilizer.

Venus flytraps grow in only one small part of the southeastern United States. They are rare now because people have drained many of the marshes where they once lived.

SNAP!

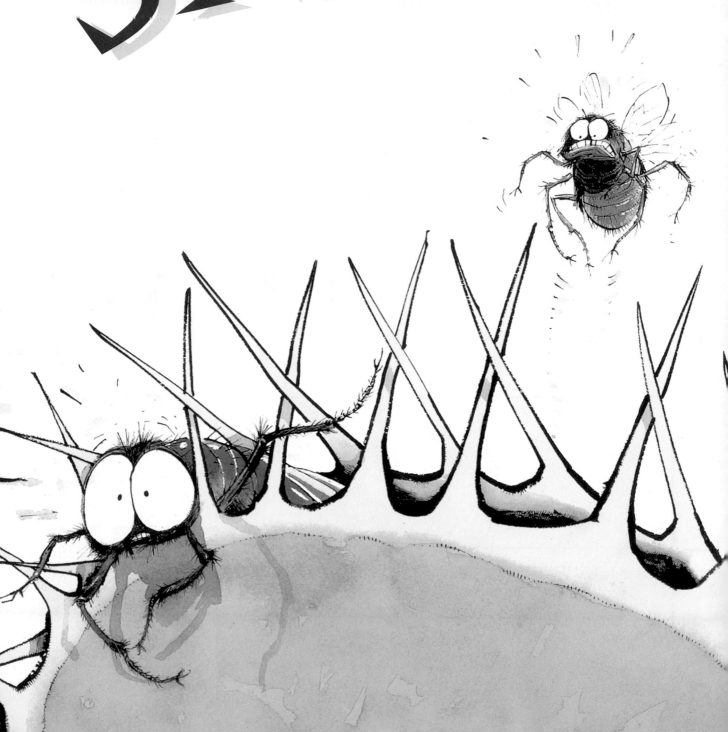

Small insects such as ants
can escape from a Venus
flytrap—they're not big
enough to be worth eating.

But flies and wasps are
a different story. Once
caught, the more they
struggle the tighter the
leaf presses together.

When the leaf is fully
closed, it begins to dissolve
its victim.

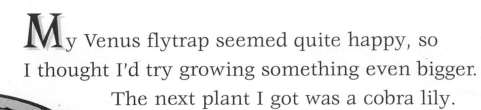

M y Venus flytrap seemed quite happy, so
I thought I'd try growing something even bigger.
The next plant I got was a cobra lily.
This one caught insects, too, but it
didn't actually do very much. It had
leaves like funnels, with a slippery
rim and a little pool at the bottom.
When insects crawled inside,
they fell into the pool and couldn't
climb out. So they stayed there and
became bug soup for the lily.

Cobra lilies get their
name because their leaves
look like cobras, not
because they eat them!

I was very happy with my cobra lily. Surely it was the biggest carnivorous plant of all. But then my friend told me about pitcher plants.

Pitchers are even bigger, she said, but they are very difficult to grow. In that case, I thought, I'll just go and find some wild ones.

So I went—

all the way to Malaysia.

Cobra lilies grow along the western coast of the United States. Their leaves can be up to 18 inches long.

And there, growing up the trees at the edge
of the jungle, were hundreds of pitcher plants.
Fat red ones, thin yellow ones, curly green ones,
all waiting for flies.

I didn't see the biggest pitcher plant of all,
though. It's called the Rajah pitcher plant and it
grows on the tallest mountain in Borneo.

It has pitchers the size of footballs. People say
it can even catch some kinds of squirrels, but I'm
not convinced.

Pitcher plants are found in tropical countries. Like most other carnivorous plants, they usually grow where there is hardly any soil or where the soil is very poor.

The pitchers' leaves look like vases, and they catch insects in the same way that cobra lilies do.

There are some kinds of spiders, and even some small tree frogs, that are able to live inside the pitchers. They cling to the slippery sides and grab the insects that fall in.

One day I'll go and see for myself. . . .

The mountain is called Kinabalu. It is over 13,000 feet high. The Rajah pitcher plant only grows there and it's even rarer than the Venus flytrap.

About the Author
Martin Jenkins

Fly Traps! Plants That Bite Back is one of Martin Jenkins's first books for children. "It is absolutely autobiographical," Mr. Jenkins says about the book. He really travels to faraway jungles in search of unusual plants. Mr. Jenkins is a conservation biologist who writes articles for the World Wildlife Federation. He also is the author of *Wings, Stings and Wriggly Things.*

About the Illustrator
David Parkins

Drawing the pictures for *Fly Traps! Plants That Bite Back* brought back memories for David Parkins. "When I first started out as an illustrator," he says, "I did a book on wildlife and spent a year tramping around fields drawing berries and birds. So in a way, this book takes me back to my roots." Mr. Parkins has illustrated many other children's books. He lives in England.

Reader Response

Open for Discussion

Which kind of plant in *Fly Traps! Plants That Bite Back* was the most interesting to you? Why?

Comprehension Check

1. Think of one word to describe the narrator. Look back through the selection to find parts of the text that support your choice.

2. What is the most important way in which all the plants in the selection are alike? Use details from the text to explain.

3. Look back at the pictures. Some of them are funny. Some of the text is funny too. Is this a good way to present information? Use examples to tell why you think as you do.

4. Use the pictures on pages 150 and 151 as a **graphic source** to tell a friend how the bladderwort captures its food. Use your hands as well as your voice. (Graphic Sources)

5. Find the **graphic source** that shows how the cobra lily got its name. Tell how the plant and animal are alike. (Graphic Sources)

Test Prep

Look Back and Write

Look back at pages 155–157. Explain what must happen for an insect to get trapped in a Venus flytrap. Use the text and pictures to support your answer.

164

 **Test Prep**

Read a How-to Article

1. Preview

- A how-to article gives step-by-step instructions on how to do something. Does the title tell you what this article will teach you to do? Read the first paragraph and look at the pictures. Now do you know what this article will teach you to do?

2. Read and Locate Information

- Read the article. Use the pictures to help you understand each step. Look for information to answer these questions: What do I do? How do I use it?

3. Think and Connect

Think about *Fly Traps! Plants That Bite Back*. Then remember what you learned in "Can You Catch Flies?"

If you made the pitcher plant in this article, do you think you could really catch flies with it? Why or why not?

Can You Catch Flies?

by Rhonda Lucas Donald

A real pitcher plant catches lots of flies. If you follow these directions, you can make your own pitcher plant. Then see if you can catch flies too.

What You Need

- 6-inch × 9-inch piece of thin cardboard (about the thickness of a manila folder)
- 11-inch piece of thin string or thread
- scissors
- two strips of paper, each 3/4 inch × 4 inches
- pen or pencil
- white glue
- tape (optional)
- crayons, markers, or paints and paintbrushes

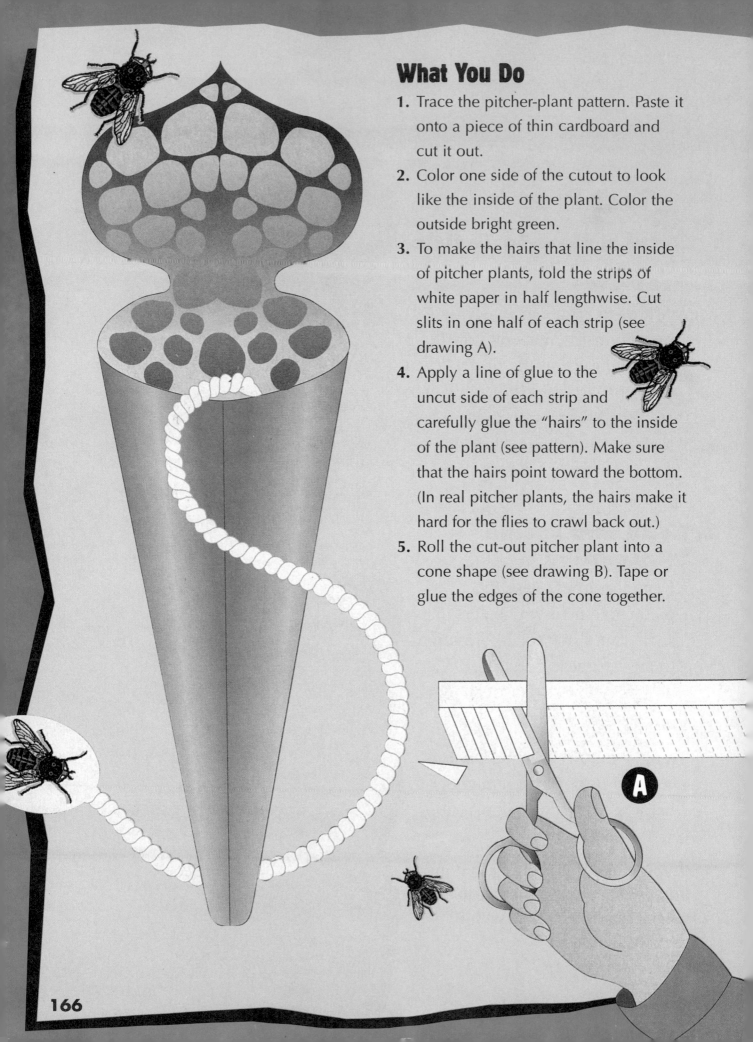

What You Do

1. Trace the pitcher-plant pattern. Paste it onto a piece of thin cardboard and cut it out.

2. Color one side of the cutout to look like the inside of the plant. Color the outside bright green.

3. To make the hairs that line the inside of pitcher plants, fold the strips of white paper in half lengthwise. Cut slits in one half of each strip (see drawing A).

4. Apply a line of glue to the uncut side of each strip and carefully glue the "hairs" to the inside of the plant (see pattern). Make sure that the hairs point toward the bottom. (In real pitcher plants, the hairs make it hard for the flies to crawl back out.)

5. Roll the cut-out pitcher plant into a cone shape (see drawing B). Tape or glue the edges of the cone together.

A

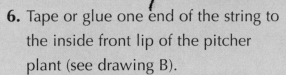

6. Tape or glue one end of the string to the inside front lip of the pitcher plant (see drawing B).

7. Trace the shapes with the flies on them. Glue each one to a piece of cardboard, draw flies on them, and cut them both out.

8. Glue the flies back-to-back onto the loose end of the string. Let them dry.

9. Now your pitcher plant is ready to catch flies! Just flip the fly up and try to get it into the pitcher.

10. When you get good at catching flies, curl the plant's "hood" down to partly cover the pitcher's opening. (Roll the hood over your finger and hold it in place for a couple of seconds.) Can your pitcher plant *still* catch its dinner?

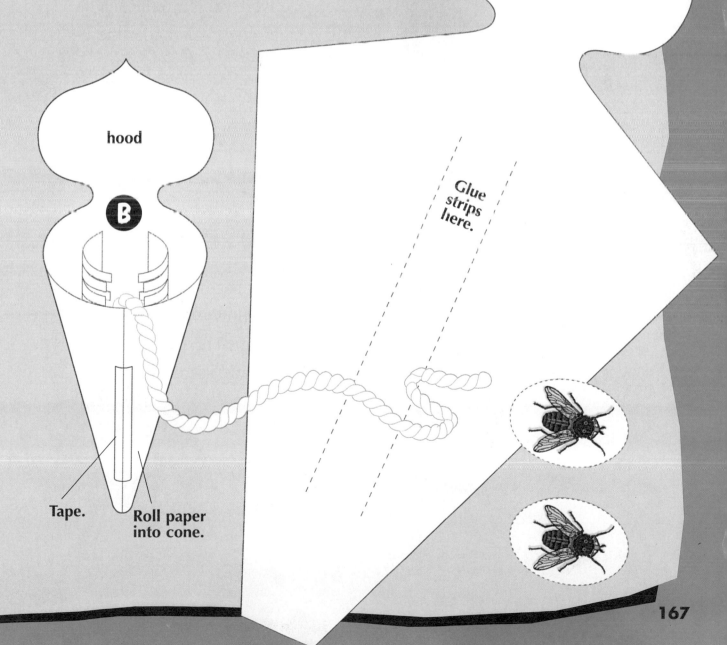

pattern

hood

B

Glue strips here.

Tape.

Roll paper into cone.

Skill Lesson

Realism and Fantasy

- A **realistic story** tells about something that could happen in real life.

- A **fantasy** has some things that could happen and some things that could not happen.

Read "Under the Umbrella" from *The Willow Umbrella* by Christine Widman and "The Naughty Umbrella" from *Roger's Umbrella* by Daniel Pinkwater.

Write About It

1. In columns labeled *realistic* and *fantasy,* write story details that show whether the story is realistic or a fantasy.

2. Which story is realistic and which is a fantasy? Tell why you think so.

UNDER
the Umbrella

by Christine Widman

Ashley sees Rebecca coming down the street. She's holding a yellow umbrella. It looks like the sun Ashley painted in her picture. She wishes Rebecca were bringing the sun so they could play dolls under the willow tree.

Rain, rain go away. Ashley wants to play.

She waves to Rebecca. "Hurry up . . . come in. We have to play inside today."

"No we don't. Come out! Let's walk in the rain."

Ashley squeezes close to Rebecca under the yellow umbrella. The air is wet and warm. The sidewalk is shiny like a gray satin sash.

THE NAUGHTY Umbrella

by Daniel Pinkwater

When Roger left for school on rainy days, or days that looked like they might be rainy, his mother always said to him, "Roger, be sure to take your umbrella."

He didn't like taking his umbrella. For one thing, it got in the way. And for another, he didn't like the way the umbrella behaved.

Sometimes the umbrella would suddenly turn itself inside out for no reason.

Sometimes it would catch a gust of wind and make Roger walk on tiptoe.

Sometimes it would even lift him completely off the ground.

But that was nothing compared to what the umbrella would do at night.

It would suddenly pop open and hop around the room. It would flap like a big bird or bat. It would try to escape out the window.

Roger would have to grab the umbrella and struggle with it until he could finally stuff it into his closet, where it would thump and flap for hours.

LOOK AHEAD

Guys from Space is about a boy who suddenly leaves his own backyard and travels very far. Could it be real? Is it a fantasy? Read and find out.

169

Vocabulary

Words to Know

breathe	planet	space
dream	scary	spaceship

Words with opposite meaning, like *hot* and *cold*, are called **antonyms**. You can often figure out the meaning of a word you don't know by finding a clue in the words around it. Sometimes this clue is an antonym.

Read this paragraph. Notice how *calm* helps you understand what *scary* means.

Was It Just a Dream?

I had a great dream! A spaceship landed outside my window. An alien asked me if I wanted to go to his planet. We flew through space at top speed. The trip wasn't calm—it was scary! What if I couldn't breathe on the strange planet? Just when I found out the planet was safe . . . I woke up!

Write About It

Imagine you traveled to another planet. Write a postcard home. Use some vocabulary words.

Guys
from
Space

written and illustrated by Daniel Pinkwater

I was in the backyard.

I wasn't doing anything.

There was something in the sky.

I looked up.

There was something big up there.

It was not a bird.

It was not an airplane.

It was not a balloon.

It was not a cloud.

It was something from space.

It was neat!

It was coming down.

It was coming down into the yard!

It did not make a noise.

It landed like a dream.

"This is good!" I said.

I was not scared.

When the thing from space had landed, a little door opened.

Guys from space came out.

They were no bigger than me.

"Is this Chicago?" they asked me.

"This is my yard," I said.

The guys from space talked to each other.

"Kid, would you like to come for a ride?"

"No!" I said.

"You don't want to come?"

"No."

"It will be fun," the space guys said. "We will bring you back."

"Nothing doing," I said.

"You will be the first Earth person to ride in our spaceship," they said.

"I am not allowed to go with anybody," I said. "Unless my mother or father says I can."

"Are your mother or father the same size as you?" the guys from space asked.

"Bigger," I said.

"Then they will not fit. Just you come."

"I have to ask my mother," I said.

"Is she scary?" the space guys wanted to know.

"Not very."

"All right, ask her. Where is she?"

"She's in the house," I said. "Wait here."

I went inside the house.

My mother was in the basement.

She was weaving.

She weaves.

She was weaving some sort of rug.

She has this loom.

It's what you weave on.

"There are some space guys in the yard," I said.

"That's nice," my mother said.

"Is it all right if I go up in the spaceship?"

"Sure," my mother said.

"Do you want to see the space guys?"

"Not right now, dear," my mother said. "I'm just doing the hard part of this rug."

"Then I can just go with them?"

"If you aren't late for supper."

"I'll see you later," I said.

"Have a good time," my mother said.

I went out into the yard.

"She says I can go," I said.

"Good!" the guys from space said.
"Get your space helmet."

"I don't have one," I said.

"No space helmet? That's too bad."

"Don't you have an extra one?" I asked.

"Afraid not."

"Then I can't go?"

"Well, you have to have a space helmet."

"Oh," I said.

"Maybe we could fix something up. What's that?"

"That's the dog's water bowl," I said.

"What's that stuff in it?"

"Water," I said.

"Could you dump it out?" they asked.

"I guess so," I said. "Would that work as a space helmet?"

"Try it on," the space guys said.

I tried it on. "It's cold," I said. "How does it look?"

"It looks good," the space guys said. "Come on."

"Why do I have to wear this?" I asked.

"You have to. It's a rule. Let's go."

We went through the little door.

The space guys turned knobs.

They pushed buttons.

They switched switches.

Something buzzed.

Something beeped.

Something whistled.

"Here we go," the space guys said. "Look out the window."

I looked out the window.

We were going up.

"Isn't this neat?" the space guys said.

We were going fast.

"Where are we going?" I asked.

"We will visit some other planet," the space guys said.

"Will I be home in time for supper?" I asked.

"What time is supper?"

"Six."

"Easy."

"I thought other planets were far away," I said.

"They are."

"How can we go to another planet and be back by six?"

"Easy. We go fast. Hold on."

The spaceship went faster.

It went very fast.

It went very, very fast.

It went faster than sound.

It went faster than light.

I didn't like it.

"This is too fast," I said.

"Never mind. We have come to a planet," the space guys said.

"What planet is this?" I asked.

"Who knows? Some planet," the guys from space said. "Let's get out and look around."

"How do you know if there is air on this planet?" I asked.

"If there is no air, you can't breathe," the space guys said.

"Then what?" I asked.

"Then we run back into the spaceship and close the door," the guys from space said.

"How about wild animals and bad people?" I asked.

"Same thing. We run back inside."

"It sounds simple."

"We are space guys. We know what we are doing."

The space guys opened the door, and we went outside.

"The air is good," the space guys said.

"I don't see any wild animals," I said.

"No, this is a good planet. We can tell," the space guys said.

"What do we do now?" I asked.

"We look around. We explore."

We looked around.

It was a neat planet.

There were a lot of rocks.

I picked one up.

"Put me down!" the rock said.

I put it down.

"The rock talked," I said.

"Hello, rock," the space guys said. "We like your planet."

"Who are you?" the rock asked.

"We are guys from space," the space guys said. "We are just visiting."

"Oh, that's all right," the rock said. "Look around and have a nice time."

"Thank you," the space guys said. "Is there anything special here? Something we should see?"

"There is a root beer stand," the rock said.

"Oh, good! We like root beer," the space guys said.

"Do you like root beer?" they asked me.

"Sure," I said.

"Where is the root beer stand?" they asked the rock.

"It is there, behind that big rock," the rock said.

We went to the root beer stand.

It was nice.

It had lots of lights.

Space things were drinking root beer.

There was a big space thing in the root beer stand.

He was ugly, in a nice way.

"Five root beers, please," the guys from space said.

"You have money?" the big space thing said.

"We have plastic fish," the space guys said. "We use plastic fish for money."

"Plastic fish are fine," the big space thing said. "Five root beers for five plastic fish."

"On our planet, we get ten root beers for five plastic fish," the space guys said.

"Do you get ice cream in the root beers?" the big space thing asked.

"No. We never heard of ice cream in root beer," the space guys said.

"Five plastic fish for five root beers with ice cream," the big space thing said.

The space guys gave the space thing five plastic fish.

"Ice cream in root beer," they said. "What a strange idea!"

The big space thing gave us the root beers with ice cream.

"This is good," the space guys said. "We will teach the people on our own planet about this."

I drank my root beer.

I ate the ice cream with a spoon.

I looked at the space things having root beer.

It was good root beer.

"Hurry and finish," the space guys said.

"We have to go?" I asked.

"We want to go to our own planet. We want to tell our people about ice cream in root beer. We want to go back and tell them before someone else does."

"You will take me home first?" I said.

"Yes. Now finish your root beer and ice cream."

I finished my root beer and ice cream.

We got into the spaceship.

The space guys took me home.

We landed in the backyard.

"Do you want to come in?" I asked the space guys. "Do you want to meet my mother?"

"Not now," the space guys said. "We want to go home. We want to tell our people."

"You want to tell them about root beer and ice cream."

"Yes! Our people will like it. We will be heroes."

"Thank you for the ride, and the root beer," I said.

"You are welcome," the space guys said.

"Good-bye."

"Good-bye."

The spaceship took off.

I went into the house.

"Why do you have the dog's water bowl on your head?" my mother asked.

"I used it for a space helmet," I said.

"Fill it with water and put it back," my mother said. "The dog may want a drink. Then wash your hands and face and come to supper."

"I took a ride in a spaceship," I said.

"That's nice, dear," my mother said. "Did you have a good time?"

"The space guys bought me a root beer," I said.

"I hope you thanked them," my mother said.

"I did," I said.

About the Author/Illustrator
Daniel Manus Pinkwater

When Daniel Manus Pinkwater was a young boy, he and his friends acted out the adventure stories they read. One day they would act out the story *20,000 Leagues Under the Sea.* The next day they might act out *The Three Musketeers.* He and his friends would tell each other about books they liked.

Now that Mr. Pinkwater is grown up, he creates his own adventure stories. He often draws the pictures for them too. Unusual things happen in his stories, such as a train car turning into a time machine and a blue moose getting a job as a waiter.

Even though amusing things happen in Mr. Pinkwater's stories, he is very serious about what he does. "I think children's books are the most important thing you can do," he says, "because these are people who are learning about reading."

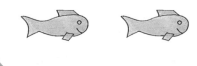

Reader Response

Open for Discussion

If guys from space landed at your house, would you want to go for a ride with them? Tell why or why not.

Comprehension Check

1. Look back on page 178. Is the space guys' plan to see whether a planet's air is okay a good one? Why or why not?

2. Look back on pages 175–176. Why does the boy wear the dog's dish as a helmet? Does the dog dish do anything that a real helmet does?

3. Does the boy's mother think he has gone on a ride in a spaceship? Use the text on pages 174–175 and page 183 to explain your answer.

4. *Guys from Space* is a **fantasy** because many things that happen in the story could not really happen. Name two events from the story that could not really happen. (Realism and Fantasy)

5. Some events in a **fantasy** could really happen. Which character seems to do only real things? What are these things? (Realism and Fantasy)

Test Prep

Look Back and Write

Look back at pages 180–182. Why do you think the space guys thought telling their own people about ice cream in root beer was so important? Use the text to help you explain.

Special Effects

By Anne Cottringer

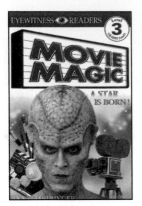

CAZ WON THE PART of Zanuck in a science fiction movie. She was on the set in costume. She had shot one scene in the morning.

After lunch Caz had a second scene where she waves goodbye to Zara, who is flying away in her spaceship. However, when she got to the set, instead of vehicles and buildings there was just a large blue wall.

"This is going to look pretty bare!" said Caz. "Is that blue wall supposed to be the sky?"

"No," smiled Kirsty, who had come to look after Caz. "This is where the magic comes in! That blue screen acts like a blank background for the scene. Later the director and special effects people will put in the background."

After they filmed the scene, Kirsty took Caz to a studio where a model maker showed them a small-scale version of Zara's spaceship flying through the sky.

"We're filming this model," explained the model maker. "Then, using a computer, we'll combine it with the scene you've just been in. We'll also add a

This astronaut is filmed in front of a blue screen, ready to go anywhere.

Things heat up for the astronaut when this background of a volcanic landscape is added.

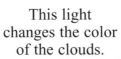

A night out on the town is also fun!

This light changes the color of the clouds.

The model is suspended in a water tank.

This light colors the bottom of the spacecraft.

larger model of the spaceport as a background. But we need to have a blue screen behind you for it to work."

"That's brilliant!" cried Caz. "Could you do some movie magic so that Zanuck goes with Zara after all?"

"Sure! We could film you in front of the blue screen clinging on to something, put it together with Zara's spaceship—and you would be flying through space hanging on to the wing of the spaceship!"

Different gels create different lighting effects.

"I'm not sure I'd like to travel that way!" laughed Caz.

Next, Kirsty took Caz to see the fierce dragon that guards the magic crystal. But the only dragon Caz could see was a sort of skeleton on a computer screen.

"It's called a wire frame," explained the woman at the computer. "We create an image of the dragon on the computer first and then use a software program to mold the dragon's muscles and paint in the skin."

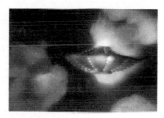

A high-speed camera shoots in close-up.

"But how does Zara get to fight the dragon if it's on a screen?" asked Caz.

"The dragon is programmed to move, and special effects experts then combine this computer image with the scene of Zara in the maze," she said.

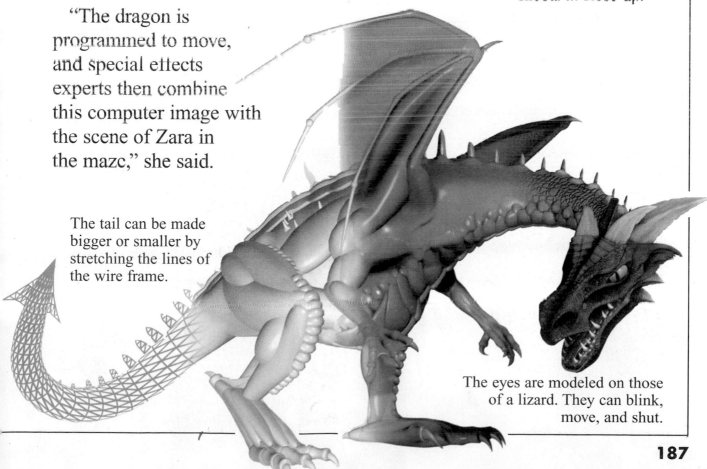

The tail can be made bigger or smaller by stretching the lines of the wire frame.

The eyes are modeled on those of a lizard. They can blink, move, and shut.

Skill Lesson

Context Clues

- To figure out the meaning of a word, use **context clues**.

- Often a context clue defines or explains the word. Look in the sentences or paragraph around the word.

- You may need to use a dictionary or glossary to check the meaning of the word.

Read "Stormy Weather" from *Weather* by Martha Ryan.

Talk About It

1. Tell what words or sentences help you understand the meanings of these words: *hurricane*, *eye*, and *tornado*.

2. Look up each word in the glossary. Do the definitions give you more or less information than the context clues in "Stormy Weather"?

Stormy Weather
by Martha Ryan

Hurricanes are bad summer storms. They usually get started out in the Atlantic Ocean.

The winds can blow up to 200 miles (322 kilometers) an hour.

Hurricane viewed from outer space

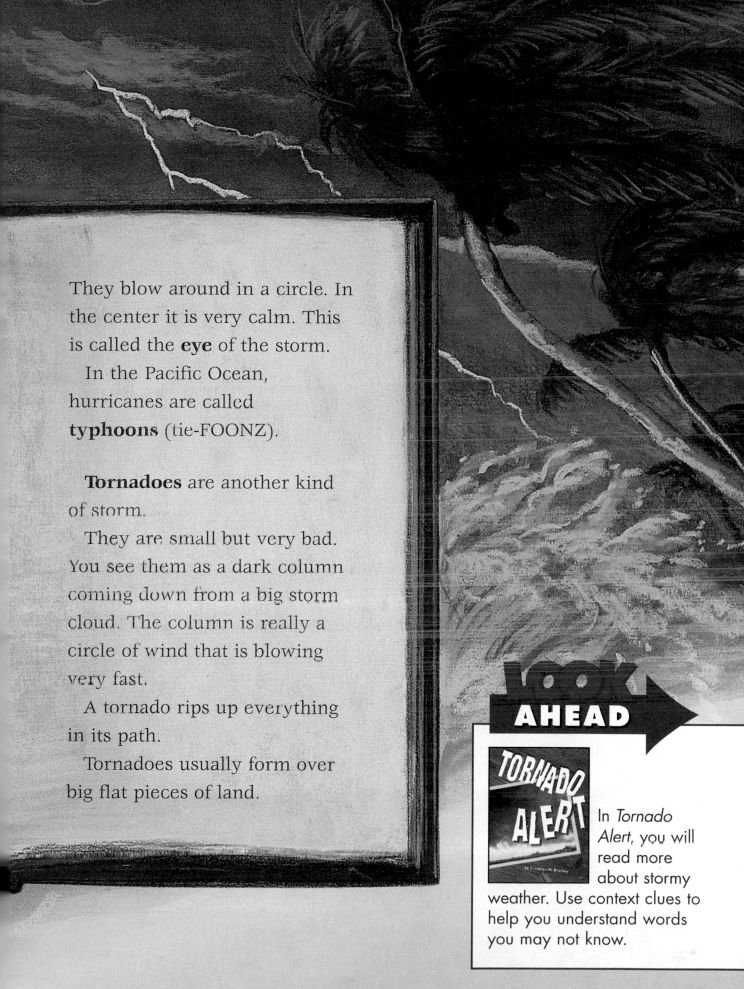

They blow around in a circle. In the center it is very calm. This is called the **eye** of the storm.

In the Pacific Ocean, hurricanes are called **typhoons** (tie-FOONZ).

Tornadoes are another kind of storm.

They are small but very bad. You see them as a dark column coming down from a big storm cloud. The column is really a circle of wind that is blowing very fast.

A tornado rips up everything in its path.

Tornadoes usually form over big flat pieces of land.

LOOK AHEAD

TORNADO ALERT

by Franklyn M. Branley

In *Tornado Alert,* you will read more about stormy weather. Use context clues to help you understand words you may not know.

Vocabulary

Words to Know

destroy   storms   noise
warnings   powerful   wrecked

Words with similar meanings, like *dish*
and *plate,* are **synonyms**. You can often
figure out the meaning of a word you
don't know by finding a clue in
the words around it. Sometimes
this clue is a synonym.

Read this paragraph. Notice how
smash helps you understand what
destroy means.

Wild Weather

A loud <u>noise</u> and winds with blowing dust are
two <u>warnings</u> of a tornado. Tornadoes are
<u>storms</u> that are very <u>powerful</u>. They can smash
windows and cars and <u>destroy</u> homes. They can
pull trees out of the ground. If a tornado is
coming, go to your basement or a room without
windows. Your house may be <u>wrecked</u>, but you
will be safe.

Talk About It

Think of a sentence about a tornado
that uses some vocabulary words.
Share your sentence with the class.

TORNADO ALERT

by Franklyn M. Branley

Tornadoes are powerful storms.

On a tornado day the air is hot and still. Clouds build up rapidly. They get thick and dark. In the distance there is thunder and lightning, rain and hail.

Here and there parts of the clouds seem to reach toward the ground. Should these parts grow larger and become funnel shaped, watch out. The funnels could become tornadoes.

The funnel of a tornado is usually dark gray or black. It may also be yellowish or red.

The colors come from red and yellow dirt picked up by the tornado as it moves along the ground.

Tornadoes can strike almost anywhere, but usually they happen where there is a lot of flat land. Most tornadoes occur in Texas, Oklahoma, Kansas, Nebraska, Iowa, and Missouri. Florida also has a lot of tornadoes.

Tornadoes can touch down over seas and lakes. When that happens, they are called waterspouts.

Most tornadoes occur during April, May, and June. That's when cold air meets warm air near the Earth's surface. The cold air pushes under the warm air. The warm air is lighter than the cold air and rises rapidly.

As the warm air moves upward, it spins around, or twists. That's why tornadoes are sometimes called twisters. Some people call them cyclones. The wind speed around the funnel of the tornado may reach 300 miles an hour. No other wind on Earth blows that fast.

As the hot air rises, it also spreads out. It makes a funnel of air, with the small part of the funnel touching the ground and the large part in the dark clouds. Air all around the tornado moves in toward the funnel. At the same time, storm winds push the twisting funnel, moving it along the Earth.

During tornado season in the United States, there may be 40 or 50 tornadoes in one week. Sometimes there are many more. Most are small. Usually a tornado blows itself out in less than an hour. Some last only a few seconds.

Small tornadoes don't travel far, and they cause little damage. Big tornadoes destroy everything in their paths. They may travel two hundred miles and last several hours.

During a tornado there is thunder and lightning, rain and hail. And there is lots of noise. It can sound as loud as a freight train or a jet engine. The word *tornado* comes from a Latin word that means "thunder." Some of the noise does come from thunder, but most of it comes from the roaring wind. There is lots of noise, and lots and lots of wind.

Tornadoes are very powerful, and some cause a lot of damage. Tornadoes can pick up branches and boards, stones and bricks, cars, and sometimes even people.

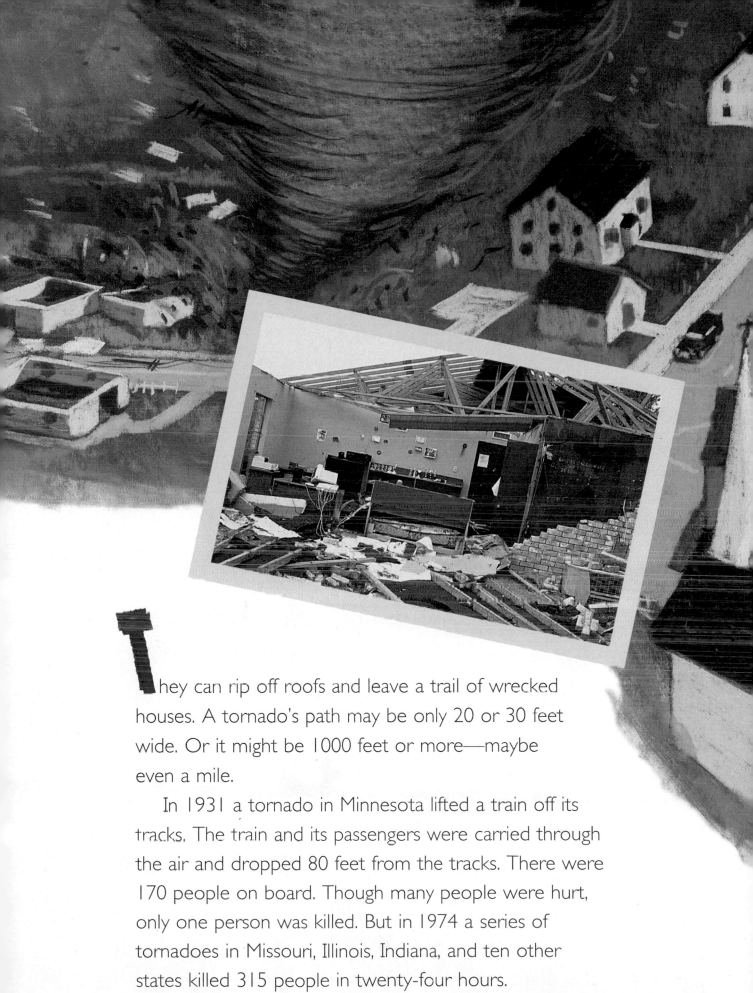

They can rip off roofs and leave a trail of wrecked houses. A tornado's path may be only 20 or 30 feet wide. Or it might be 1000 feet or more—maybe even a mile.

In 1931 a tornado in Minnesota lifted a train off its tracks. The train and its passengers were carried through the air and dropped 80 feet from the tracks. There were 170 people on board. Though many people were hurt, only one person was killed. But in 1974 a series of tornadoes in Missouri, Illinois, Indiana, and ten other states killed 315 people in twenty-four hours.

Scientists keep a close watch during tornado season. They use satellites that see storms developing. And there is radar to detect tornadoes.

Tornado spotters are people who watch for tornadoes. They tell radio and television stations to warn people about tornadoes while the twisters are still far away. The warnings tell people to go to a safe spot, where the tornado can't hurt them.

If a tornado is on its way, here's what you should do. Go to a nearby storm cellar. Storm cellars are underground rooms with heavy doors. They are safe.

If you are in a mobile home, get out of it. A tornado can rip apart a mobile home, even when it is tied down with strong cables. Lie facedown in a ditch and cover your head with your hands. When you're in a ditch, sticks and stones flying through the air can't hit you.

If you are in a house, go to the basement and crouch under the stairs or under a heavy workbench. Or go to a closet that is far from an outside wall. Be sure to keep far away from windows. The wind could smash them and send splinters of glass through the air.

If you are in school, follow directions. Your teacher will take you to a basement or to an inside hall. Crouch on your knees near an inner wall. Bend over and clasp your hands behind your head. Most important, keep away from glass windows.

If you are out in the country in a car, don't try to race the tornado. Get out, and find a ditch to lie in.

When there's a tornado, there is also thunder and lightning. So keep away from metal things and from anything that uses electricity. Lightning can travel along metal pipes, and also along electric and telephone wires.

Listen to a battery radio. The radio will tell you when the storm has passed by. Stay where you are safe until you are sure the tornado is over.

Tornadoes are scary. Even if you are not right in the funnel, there is heavy rain all around, dark skies, thunder, lightning, and lots of wind. Often there will be hailstones. They may be as big as golf balls, or even bigger.

Don't panic. Know what to do when there is a tornado. And know where to go.

There is no way to stop tornadoes. But you can be safe from them when you know what to do.

About the Author

Franklyn M. Branley

When Franklyn M. Branley started teaching long ago, not many students your age studied science. Since Mr. Branley was interested in science, he started teaching it to his fourth-graders. Other teachers liked his ideas so much that he wrote instructions on how to teach science. Before long, he was writing science books for children too.

Mr. Branley believes that authors of nonfiction books are like teachers. "They write so that readers will better understand whatever the subject may be," he says. "Also, the writer hopes the book has prodded the reader into thinking and wondering."

You might enjoy reading some of Mr. Branley's books about space. He has written several about our solar system including *Floating in Space* and *The Planets in Our Solar System, Stage 2*.

Reader Response

Open for Discussion

Think of a bad storm you have been in or one that someone has told you about. How was it like or unlike a tornado described in *Tornado Alert?* What was it like to be in it?

Comprehension Check

1. What is the author explaining with the diagram on page 196? Use the text and picture to explain your answer.

2. Look back on pages 194 and 195. Several real storms are described. Choose one and make up a newspaper headline for it. Use details in the text to help you.

3. Look back at page 201. Several places are described as safer during a tornado. Why are most of them underground? Find facts in the selection to support your answer.

4. Find the word *waterspouts* on page 194. Tell what **context clues** gave you the meaning of the word. (Context Clues)

5. Find the word *crouch* on page 201. Tell what **context clues** gave you the meaning of the word. (Context Clues)

 **Test Prep**

Look Back and Write

Look at the pictures and text on pages 198–199. Explain the kind of damage a tornado can do.

Myths About Tornadoes

from *Kids Discover*

Before 1952, the National Weather Service was not allowed to use the word *tornado* in its forecasts for fear of panic. Tornadoes are scary storms, but they are less scary when some of the myths about them are debunked—by scientists.

MYTH:

When you see a tornado coming, you should get into your car and try to outrun it.

TRUTH:

Cars can become snarled in clogged intersections and stopped by downed trees and power lines, leaving passengers totally vulnerable. Seek shelter in a basement, a small closet, or a bathroom in the center of your house on the lowest floor.

MYTH:

It always hails before a tornado.

TRUTH:

Sometimes hail occurs before a tornado, sometimes after, and sometimes not at all.

Amazing Occurrences

A tornado lifted up a child and deposited him— unharmed—in a tree. ▼

A plane wing was carried 35 miles, perhaps the heaviest piece of debris carried that far. ▼

◀ A check was found in a cornfield, 305 miles away, the longest known distance that debris has ever been carried.

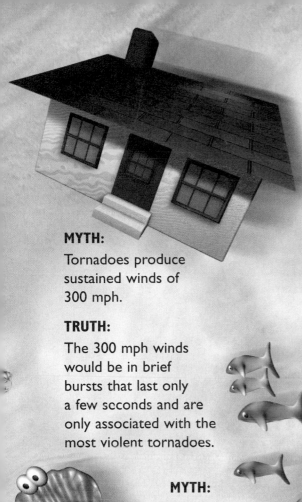

MYTH:

Tornadoes produce sustained winds of 300 mph.

TRUTH:

The 300 mph winds would be in brief bursts that last only a few seconds and are only associated with the most violent tornadoes.

MYTH:

It can't rain fish.

TRUTH:

It can rain fish—or frogs or snails or salamanders—if the water in which the animals dwell is blown horizontally and becomes embodied in the spiraling upward flow of a tornado. The water may rise up in the column to the cloud base. When the updraft weakens, the animals—along with other debris—fall out, with the rain.

◄ A pair of trousers was carried 39 miles, with $95 remaining in a pocket.

Horses, hitched to a rail, were lifted from their farm and carried a quarter of a mile. All were found unhurt ◄ and hitched to the same rail.

MYTH:

Our town is protected from tornadoes.

TRUTH:

No town is protected. An intense tornado knows no boundaries. Tornadoes are not deterred by hills. They're not even deterred by mountains three thousand feet high.

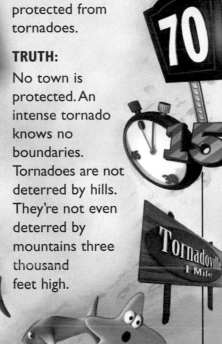

Facts About Tornadoes

Typical speed: 30–35 mph, but some move at speeds up to 70 mph

Typical time: Under 15 minutes, but some have lasted as long as an hour

Typical path for all tornadoes: Under 50 yards wide and under one mile long

Intensity: More than half have winds below 110 mph. A little more than one percent are rated as violent, with winds exceeding 200 mph.

Movement: Most tornadoes travel from southwest to northeast.

Damage: In the past century, tornadoes in North America have killed between 15,000 and 20,000 people and injured many more.

Property loss: Average of one billion dollars per year

Fact and Opinion

- A **statement of fact** can be proved true or false.

- A **statement of opinion** is what someone believes or thinks. There may or may not be a good reason to think this way.

- Words that express what someone feels or thinks are clues that a statement is an opinion. Look for clue words such as *believe*, *like*, and *should*.

Read "About Sharks" by Don C. Reed from *Boys' Life* magazine.

Talk About It

1. What is one statement of fact that you find in the article about sharks? Share your fact with a classmate.

2. What is one opinion about sharks that the author has? How do you know this is an opinion?

About SHARKS

by Don C. Reed

Sharks are as natural to the sea as sparrows are to the sky. They live in every neighborhood of the ocean, from warm tropic waters to the chilly depths. The Greenland shark lives among and beneath the Arctic Ice.

When I worked as a diver for an aquarium-zoo in California, I spent 11,000 hours underwater, often near sharks.

I like sharks. I believe they are worth saving. As predators, sharks help keep the

ocean healthy. They eat weak and sick fish, because those are the easiest to catch. This keeps fish disease from spreading, wiping out whole schools. In this way, sharks help other fish survive. Fish are a valuable source of food for humans and for livestock (fish meal is used to make cattle and chicken feed). Sharks protect our fish supply.

Sharks themselves make good eating for people, because they have no bones. (Their skeletons are made of cartilage, or gristle.) We can take a limited number of sharks for food without threatening them.

LOOK AHEAD

DANGER— ICEBERGS!

In *Danger—Icebergs!*, discover how icebergs affect the oceans where fish and sharks live. Watch for clue words to know which are statements of opinion.

Vocabulary

Words to Know

alert	ocean	thousands
breaks	melt	

Many words have more than one meaning. To decide which meaning is correct, look for clues in nearby sentences.

Read the ship's log. Pay special attention to its whole meaning. Decide whether *breaks* means "broken places" or "comes apart."

First Mate's Log

It's my job to look out for icebergs. I have to be alert because icebergs could hurt our ship. An iceberg can be thousands of feet long before it breaks into smaller pieces. All icebergs melt, but melting can take a long time. If our ship hits one of the big icebergs, it could sink into the ocean. Everyone on the ship depends on me.

Write About It

An iceberg is floating in front of the ship. Tell what happens next. Use some of the vocabulary words.

DANGER– ICEBERGS!

by Roma Gans

Year after year, snow falls in the North. It falls on Alaska, Canada, Siberia, and Greenland. It also falls on the South Pole in Antarctica—where the penguins are.

Even the summer is cold in those places, so the snow does not melt. Over thousands of years it gets packed harder and harder until it is ice. In some places the ice can be three miles deep. This big cover of ice is called a glacier.

As the ice gets thicker and thicker in the glacier, it pushes toward the ocean.

The ocean waves beat hard against it. They make deep cracks in the glacier. All at once, there is a loud roar as a chunk of the glacier breaks off. This great chunk of ice is an iceberg.

Thousands of icebergs break off from glaciers each year. Some are large and look like shiny mountains. Others look like big buildings. Some are very wide and flat. Entire towns could be built on them.

Bergs float away from the glacier slowly, moving only three or four miles per hour. You can walk faster than many bergs float. Ocean currents sweep them in and out of a straight line on their way to warmer waters. It may be three or four years before some bergs melt completely away.

Often, several bergs get pushed together and make an ice pack. The pack looks like a floating city of ice.

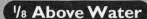
Water Level

⁷/₈ **Below Water**

Sometimes an iceberg tilts to one side. It may even turn upside down. If it touches bottom, its high peaks will be scraped away. Sometimes little bergs may break off a big berg.

Sailors can see only the tops of bergs. About one-eighth of a berg floats above water, and about seven-eighths is hidden below. The part below stretches out deep and wide; it often has sharp edges. Ships stay far away to be safe, even from small bergs.

Holes are made in icebergs when the ice melts or is gashed out as a berg scrapes land. Seals and polar bears often crawl into these holes. Seal pups have been born in iceberg hollows. You can hear their yelps and barks.

Bubbles of air form in an iceberg, and when they break, anyone near hears a loud boom.

Hundreds of years ago there were brave sailors who crossed the Atlantic in wooden ships. They kept watch day and night. They had no telescopes or radios to guide them. They steered away from icebergs. Even when the sailors kept good watch, ships sometimes ran into icebergs and were sunk.

Even strong modern ships have struck bergs. One such crash happened in April 1912. A ship called the *Titanic* sailed from England on its first voyage. "Titanic" means large. The ship was the biggest and most beautiful ship ever built. No storms or icebergs could sink it—or so people said.

The *Titanic* leaves from England in 1912.

After four calm days of sailing, Captain E. J. Smith got radio messages that there were icebergs ahead. The ship sailed on.

Another radio alert came, but too late. There was a jerk and a grinding crash. The *Titanic* had hit an iceberg. Seams in the ship's metal hull began to give way.

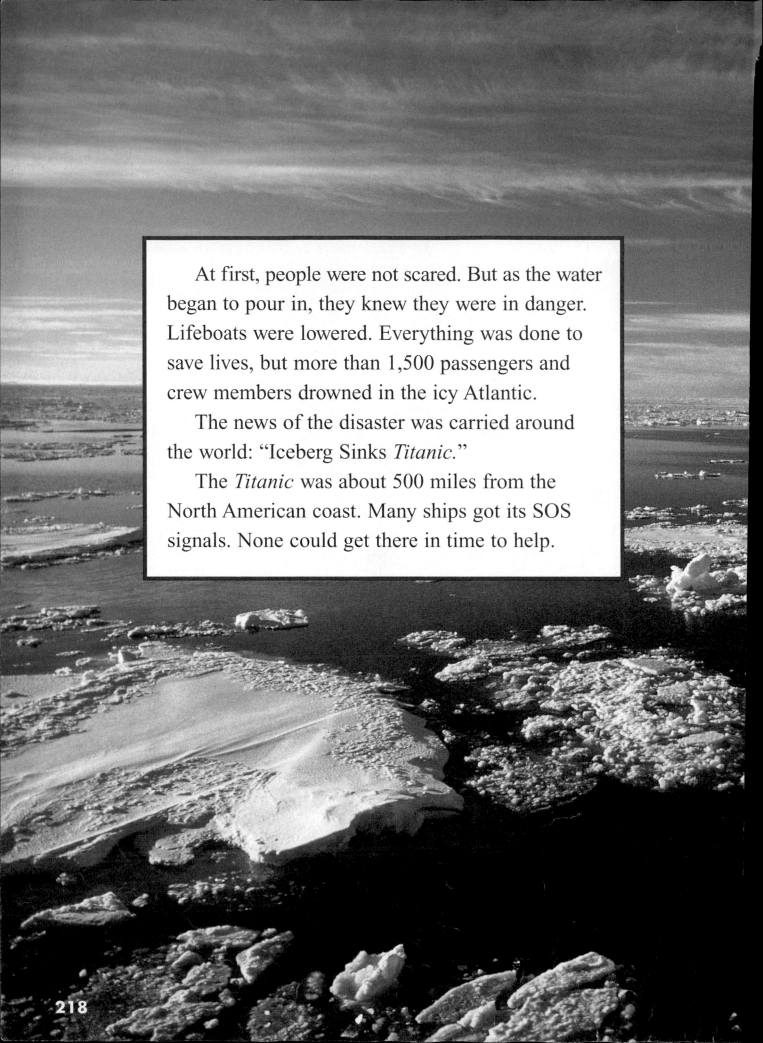

At first, people were not scared. But as the water began to pour in, they knew they were in danger. Lifeboats were lowered. Everything was done to save lives, but more than 1,500 passengers and crew members drowned in the icy Atlantic.

The news of the disaster was carried around the world: "Iceberg Sinks *Titanic.*"

The *Titanic* was about 500 miles from the North American coast. Many ships got its SOS signals. None could get there in time to help.

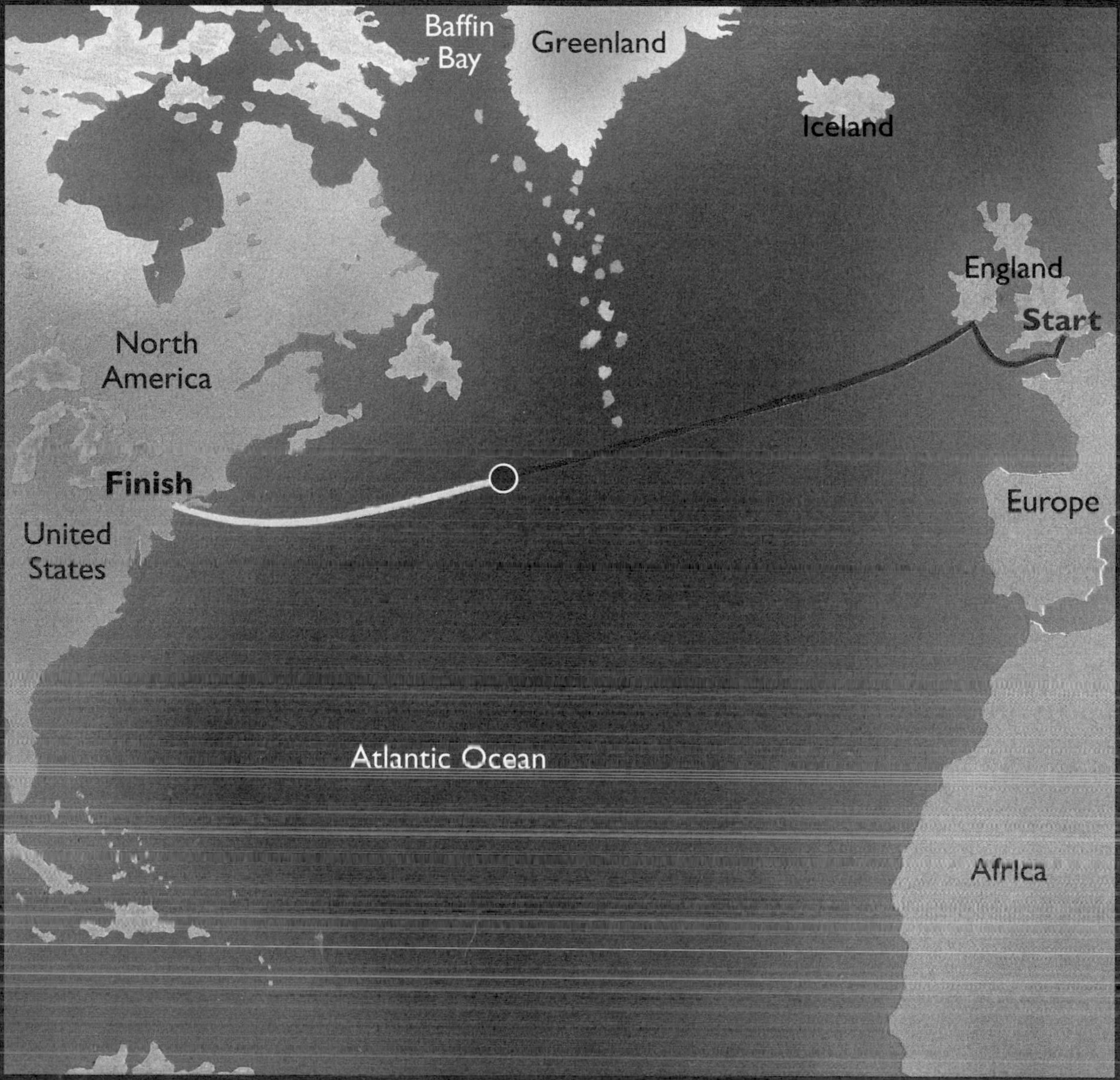

Map shows the path of the *Titanic* and where it hit the iceberg and sank.

The berg that sank the *Titanic* was not large.
Survivors of the disaster said the berg's highest point
was about 100 feet above the water. Below water it
may have extended 500 feet down. It was almost
1,000 feet wide. The iceberg had broken off a glacier
in Greenland, on Baffin Bay. For three years it had
moved slowly south in the Atlantic with many much
larger bergs.

After the sinking of the *Titanic*, the berg drifted on.
As it moved into warmer waters, it began to melt. It
became filled with holes, and pieces broke off. It got
smaller and smaller. The last of the berg disappeared
months after the tragedy.

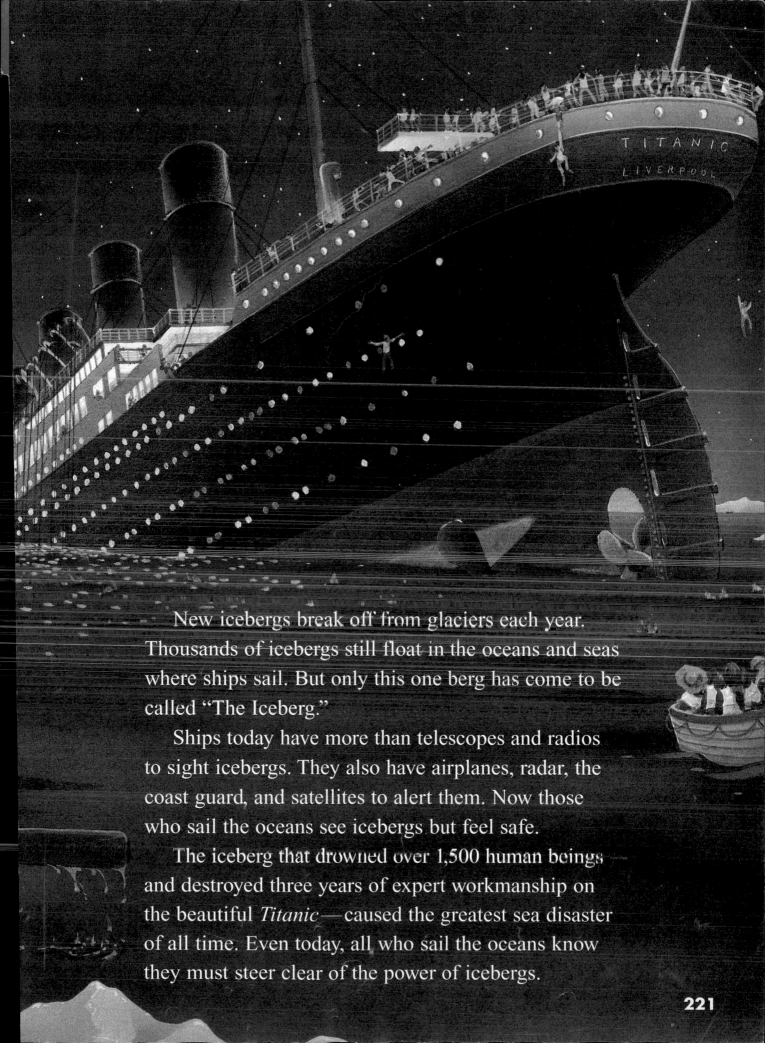

New icebergs break off from glaciers each year.
Thousands of icebergs still float in the oceans and seas
where ships sail. But only this one berg has come to be
called "The Iceberg."

Ships today have more than telescopes and radios
to sight icebergs. They also have airplanes, radar, the
coast guard, and satellites to alert them. Now those
who sail the oceans see icebergs but feel safe.

The iceberg that drowned over 1,500 human beings
and destroyed three years of expert workmanship on
the beautiful *Titanic*—caused the greatest sea disaster
of all time. Even today, all who sail the oceans know
they must steer clear of the power of icebergs.

About the Author

Roma Gans

Roma Gans didn't start writing children's books until late in her life. Before she started writing, she was a teacher and a college professor. She wrote *Danger—Icebergs!* when she was eighty-two years old.

Something Ms. Gans enjoyed more than anything was watching children learn. As she wrote, she thought about the children who would read her books. "I write and visualize faces before me who are reading as I write," she said. She loved children!

Other books by Ms. Gans that you may enjoy include *How Do Birds Find Their Way?* and *Let's Go Rock Collecting.*

Reader Response

Open for Discussion
How do you think it would feel to be on a ship and see an iceberg? Explain.

Comprehension Check

1. The author tells about the size of icebergs in several ways. She uses numbers, adjectives, and comparisons. Which way gives you the best idea of an iceberg's size? Use the text to explain.

2. One of the things that makes an iceberg dangerous is that it is much bigger than it looks. Look back at page 215 to explain why an iceberg looks smaller than it is.

3. Icebergs and tornadoes are both dangerous. Which one is more dangerous? Use details from the text to explain your answer.

4. Which sentence states a **fact,** and which states an **opinion?** (Fact and Opinion)
   - The *Titanic* was the most beautiful ship ever built.
   - When it was built, the *Titanic* was the biggest ship ever built.

5. Tell a **fact** about icebergs. Tell an **opinion** about them. (Fact and Opinion)

 Test Prep

Look Back and Write

Look back at pages 212–213. How do icebergs form? What do they look like? Use details from the text and pictures to help you explain.

GLACIER TREK

by Alan Macek as told to
Vivien Bowers
Photos by Vivien Bowers

Our guide shows me how to tie into the rope. Ropes are important tools for glacier travel. If I start to slip, the others can anchor themselves with their ice axes. Then the rope connecting us will keep me from falling.

Can you believe it? Here we are, hiking on snow and ice in the middle of summer! That's my brother, Ian, leading the way along a snowy ridge in the photo at left. And that's me bringing up the rear. Our friend, Guy, is in the middle.

Fred, our guide, is ahead of us, hollering back encouragement: "You guys are doing great!" And we feel great—as if we were walking on top of the world.

We're in a mountain range near where we live in British Columbia, Canada. These mountains are so high that the snow never melts—even in summer. (The higher you go, the colder the air is.) Instead of melting, the snow piles up in layers, year after year. Slowly it packs down to form super-thick sheets of ice called *glaciers* (GLAY-shurz).

Fred told us that glaciers flow downhill. "They're just like rivers," he explained, "except that they flow v-e-r-y slowly—maybe only a few inches a day."

LEARNING THE ROPES

"Before you start wandering around, you need to be equipped," Fred had told us, uncoiling some long, thick rope. Fred knows all about climbing on glaciers safely. He tied us to the rope and handed each of us an ice axe. The axes make handy walking sticks. But to keep from slipping down slopes, we can use the pointed ends to grip the ice.

Fred showed us how to walk on the glacier. The rope—our safety line—keeps us tied together. And now here we are, testing our new skills.

CRACKING UP

We take each step with caution. In fact, Fred won't let us go anywhere that's unsafe. A glacier can be dangerous. It can gobble people up. You think I'm joking? Then you haven't heard of a crevasse (kruh-VASS)! On our way to check one out, Fred tells us how these ice cracks form.

"If the glacier flows over a hill or is forced around a sharp corner, the ice on the surface may crack open. It's like a chunk of modeling clay that cracks or breaks if you pull or bend it too quickly."

ALL IN A SUMMER DAY

Just as we're getting the hang of glacier hiking, we're already heading back to our starting point. There's just one thing left to do. We unfasten our ropes and head to the top of a short slope that Fred says is clear of crevasses. Then we "ski" down it on the soles of our boots. We end up tumbling head over heels, landing in a snowy heap at the bottom.

Ice and snow sure are cool fun—especially in summertime.

Ian and I act as anchors while Guy peers into the gaping mouth of another deep crevasse. Without us as safeguards, Guy could fall in and be lo-o-o-ong gone!

Skill Lesson

Main Idea and Details

- The **main idea** is the most important idea of a paragraph. A main idea is sometimes stated in the paragraph.

- **Supporting details** are small pieces of information in the paragraph that tell more about the main idea.

Read "Shapes and Sizes of Sea Birds" from *Discovering Sea Birds* by Anthony Wharton.

Write About It

1. Work with a partner to write down the main idea of each paragraph. Use a separate sheet of paper for each main idea.

2. Decide what details support the main idea in each paragraph and write them under the main idea. Share your findings with other pairs.

Shapes and Sizes of Sea Birds

by Anthony Wharton

The bodies of many sea birds, such as albatrosses, penguins, and pelicans, are quite stoutly built. Others, like those of terns and petrels, are fairly slender. All of them, however, are very streamlined.

Sea birds vary a lot in size, which helps us to identify the different kinds. The smallest sea bird, a least storm petrel, is only about 13 cm (5 in.) in

puffin

gannet

cormorant

length. This is shorter than the bills of many albatrosses. The largest albatross has a wingspan of more than 360 cm (12 ft) and an emperor penguin may weigh as much as 40 kg (88 lb).

Sea birds' bills are very varied and can also help in identification. For example, most people can recognize a puffin because of its colorful, triangular bill. Pelicans, too, are easily recognized because of the shape of their pouched bills, which can hold up to 13.5 liters (3.5 gal) of water.

pelican

pacific gull

black-headed gull

AHEAD

Nights of the Pufflings

In *Nights of the Pufflings*, you can learn more about one kind of seabird—the puffin. Read and look for the details about this bird.

Vocabulary

Words to Know

burrows	hatch	cliff
searching	cardboard	
underground	island	

Words that are pronounced the same but have different spellings and meanings are **homophones**. To understand the meaning of a homophone, look for clues near it.

Read this paragraph. Why is *burrows* used below and not *burros*?

Bird Rescue

We were on an island searching for birds hurt by an oil spill. Birds living up on the cliff were safe. Others tried to go underground. They made burrows in the sand on the shore. Their holes were filled with oil. We found a nest of eggs ready to hatch. We put them in a cardboard box to take them some place safe.

Write About It

Use vocabulary words in a slogan to get people to help rescue birds.

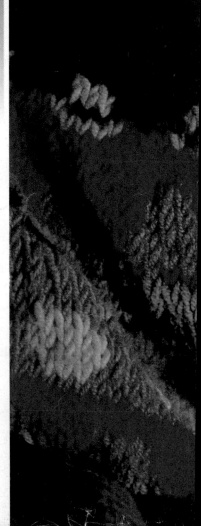

Nights of the Pufflings

photographs and text by Bruce McMillan

Heimaey Island, Iceland, April

Halla searches the sky every day. As she watches from high on a cliff overlooking the sea, she spots her first puffin of the season. She whispers to herself, "Lundi," which means "puffin" in Icelandic.

Soon the sky is speckled with them—puffins, puffins everywhere. Millions of these birds are returning from their winter at sea. They are coming back to Halla's island and the nearby uninhabited islands to lay eggs and raise puffin chicks. It's the only time they come ashore.

While Halla and her friends are at school in the
village beneath the cliffs, the puffins continue to land.
These "clowns of the sea" return to the same burrows
year after year. Once back, they busy themselves
getting their underground nests ready. Halla and all the
children of Heimaey can only wait and dream of the
nights of the pufflings yet to come.

On the weekends, Halla and her friends climb
over the cliffs to watch the birds. They see puffin pairs
tap-tap-tap their beaks together. Each pair they see
will soon tend an egg. Deep inside the cliffs that egg
will hatch a chick. That chick will grow into a young
puffling. That puffling will take its first flight. The nights
of the pufflings will come.

In the summer, while Halla splashes in the cold ocean water, the puffins also splash. The sea below the cliffs is dotted with puffins bobbing on the waves. Like Halla, many puffins that ride the waves close to the shore are young. The older birds usually fly further out to sea where the fishing is better. The grown-up puffins have to catch lots of fish, because now that it's summer they are feeding more than just themselves.

Halla's friend, Arnar Ingi, spies a puffin overhead. "Fisk," he whispers as he gazes at the returning puffin's bill full of fish. The puffin eggs have hatched, and the parents are bringing home fish to feed their chicks. The nights of the pufflings are still long weeks away, but Arnar Ingi thinks about getting some cardboard boxes ready.

Halla and her friends never see the chicks—only the chicks' parents see them. The baby puffins never come out. They stay safely hidden in the long dark tunnels of their burrows. But Halla and her friends hear them calling out for food. *"Peep-peep-peep."* The growing chicks are hungry. Their parents have to feed them—sometimes ten times a day—and carry many fish in their bills.

All summer long the adult puffins fish and tend to their feathers. By August, flowering baldusbrá blanket the burrows. With the baldusbrá in full bloom, Halla knows that the wait is over. The hidden chicks have grown into young pufflings. The pufflings are ready to fly and will at last venture out into the night. Now it's time.

It's time for Halla and her friends to get out their boxes and flashlights for the nights of the pufflings. Starting tonight, and for the next two weeks, the pufflings will be leaving for their winter at sea. Halla and her friends will spend each night searching for stranded pufflings that don't make it to the water. But the village cats and dogs will be searching too. It will be a race to see who finds the stray pufflings first. By ten o'clock the streets of Heimaey are alive with roaming children.

In the darkness of night, the pufflings leave their burrows for their first flight. It's a short, wing-flapping trip from the high cliffs. Most of the birds splash-land safely in the sea below. But some get confused by the village lights—perhaps they think the lights are moonbeams reflecting on the water. Hundreds of the pufflings crash-land in the village every night. Unable to take off from flat ground, they run around and try to hide. Dangers await. Even if the cats and dogs don't get them, the pufflings might get run over by cars or trucks.

Halla and her friends race to the rescue. Armed with their flashlights, they wander through the village. They search dark places. Halla yells out "puffling" in Icelandic. "Lundi pysja!" She has spotted one. When the puffling runs down the street, she races after it, grabs it, and nestles it in her arms. Arnar Ingi catches one, too. No sooner are the pufflings safe in the cardboard boxes than more of them land nearby. "Lundi pysja! Lundi pysja!"

For two weeks all the children of Heimaey sleep late in the day so they can stay out at night. They rescue thousands of pufflings. There are pufflings, pufflings, everywhere, and helping hands too—even though the pufflings instinctively nip at helping fingers. Every night Halla and her friends take the rescued pufflings home. The next day they send their guests on their way. Halla meets her friends and, with the boxes full of pufflings, they hike down to the beach.

It's time to set the pufflings free. Halla releases one first. She holds it up so that it will get used to flapping its wings. Then, with the puffling held snugly in her hands, she counts "Einn-tveir-ÞRÍR!" as she swings the puffling three times between her legs. The last swing is the highest, launching the bird up in the air and out over the water beyond the surf. It's only the second time this puffling has flown, so it flutters just a short distance before safely splash-landing.

Day after day Halla's pufflings paddle away, until the nights of the pufflings are over for the year. As she watches the last of the pufflings and adult puffins leave for their winter at sea, Halla bids them farewell until next spring. She wishes them a safe journey as she calls out "good-bye, good-bye" in Icelandic. "Bless, bless!"

About the Author/ Photographer
Bruce McMillan

Bruce McMillan's father gave him a camera when he was five, and he is still taking pictures. In high school, he couldn't afford his senior pictures, so he took pictures of himself to trade with friends. His pictures were different, though. "Using a top hat and some charcoal for a beard, I became Abe Lincoln," he remembers.

Reader Response

Open for Discussion

Would you like to take part in saving the pufflings? Why or why not?

Comprehension Check

1. Look at page 234. How does Arnar know that the pufflings have hatched? Use details from the text to support your answer.

2. How do Halla and her friends feel about the pufflings? Give examples from the selection to support your answer.

3. Could helping the pufflings be dangerous? Use details from the text to support your answer.

4. What is the **main idea** of the paragraph on page 239? (Main Idea and Supporting Details)

5. What **details support** that **main idea**? (Main Idea and Supporting Details)

Test Prep

Look Back and Write

Look back at page 235. The picture on the right shows a hole in the ground. What is this hole? Describe what might be in it. Use details from the story in your description.

Test Prep

How to Read an Informational Article

1. Preview

- Some magazine articles have titles and headings that tease you into reading more. They do not let you know if the article will tell facts, entertain you, or something else. Look at the pictures and captions to figure out the purpose of the article.

2. Read and Use a Web

- Read and take notes in a web to help you remember information about spoonbills.

Spoonbill

3. Think and Connect

Think about *Nights of the Pufflings*. Then look over your notes from "Spoonbill!"

How are spoonbill chicks like pufflings? How are they different?

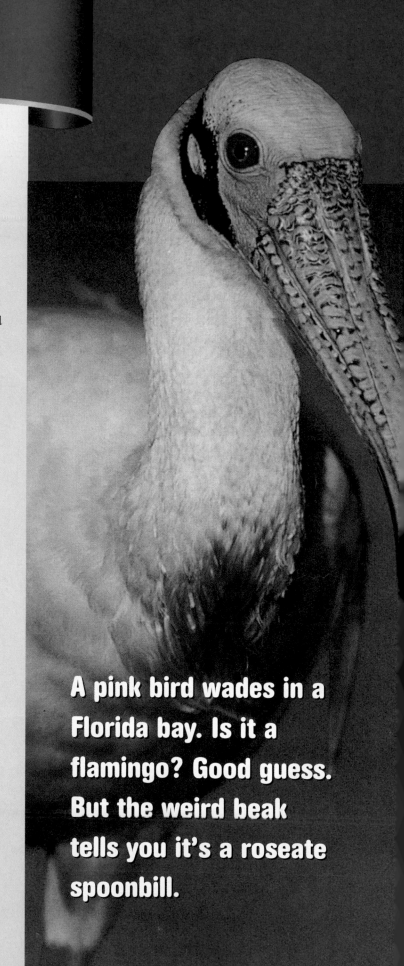

A pink bird wades in a Florida bay. Is it a flamingo? Good guess. But the weird beak tells you it's a roseate spoonbill.

You don't need a knife or fork when you're a Spoonbill!

by Cynthia Berger

Stirring Up Dinner

Other wading birds, such as herons and egrets, have beaks like swords. They spot their prey and stab it. But spoonbills often feed in muddy water where they can't see their prey. So they stir up dinner with built-in spoons.

See the bird in the picture to the right. It's swinging its spoon-shaped bill back and forth under water. The bird holds the tip of its long bill just a bit above the soft, muddy bottom. That's where tiny fish are hiding. The sweeping bill stirs up little whirlpools that lift them from the bottom. If a fish bumps against the bill, *snatch-snap!* it's trapped. Then the bird lifts its bill out of the water and gulps a spoonful of fish.

Besides eating fish, spoonbills also eat tiny shrimp and other little

How is this spoonbill feeding today? With its bill! That's how it finds prey in the muddy water. It can catch creatures by touch—without even peeking.

creatures. In the United States, the birds find these creatures in marshes near the coasts of Florida, Louisiana, and Texas.

Pretty in Pink

Can you see why roseate spoonbills are also called "flame birds"? During the breeding season, which runs from November to April, their wing feathers are a flaming pink color. They also grow yellow feathers on their sides.

Spoonbills are real show-offs when it's time to mate. Picture this: A group of birds suddenly takes

245

Teamwork

Building the nest is a team effort. The male collects sticks and passes them to his mate. Then the female builds a bowl-shaped nest in a bush or tree.

Spoonbills nest in large groups called colonies. In these noisy, smelly colonies are other long-legged wading birds too, such as herons and egrets.

Spoonfed

When the fuzzy chicks hatch, they don't have spoons of their own. Their bills are perfectly straight. And they depend on Mom or Dad to spoon up some dinner.

The chicks beg for food with whistling noises. When a parent opens its spoon-shaped bill, the chick sticks its head right inside. Then the big bird coughs up some food. This may sound gross, but it works for spoonbills!

Above: "Have another stick, honey," the male spoonbill seems to say. With sticks like that, the female can make a sturdy nest.

Inset: Yikes! What's going on here? The big bird is NOT eating its chick. The baby gets fed with food it finds wa-a-ay inside its parent's throat.

flight and circles overhead. When the birds land, they stick out their tongues. But they're not being sassy. As their tongues go out, they also stretch their necks. And that shows off the bright orange skin on their throats. It's their way to say, "Look at me. Wouldn't I make a great mate?"

Troubles and Help In Florida

Imagine having a fan made out of a spoonbill wing. Long ago, fancy ladies liked to cool themselves with fans like that. And many birds were killed to make the fans. That was the start of the birds' troubles. By one hundred years ago, spoonbills were almost gone in the United States.

Then new laws were made to protect spoonbills and other birds, and they started to make a comeback. By the 1970s, thousands of birds were nesting in Florida once again.

Troubles Today

Now spoonbills have a new problem. People aren't harming the birds on purpose. But they have been taking more and more water from the big wetland called the Everglades.

Why does it matter? Well, that water once flowed into the marshes along the coast—the marshes where the spoonbills live. Without fresh water, the little creatures that the spoonbills eat can't live in the marshes. And without spoonbill food, the spoonbills can't live there either.

More Help On the Way?

The National Wildlife Federation has been working on a great plan to help the Everglades. Other groups have helped with the plan too. If the plan is put in place and if it works, fresh water will start to flow into the marshes again. And then—hooray—there may be plenty of food for the birds with the built-in spoons!

These goofy-looking spoonbill chicks don't have their "spoons" yet. The tips of their bills will start to widen when the birds are about nine days old.

247

Clouds

by Aileen Fisher

Wonder where they come from?
Wonder where they go?
Wonder why they're sometimes high
and sometimes hanging low?
Wonder what they're made of,
and if they weigh a lot?
Wonder if the sky feels bare up there
when clouds are *not?*

THE SKY

by Lee Blair

It must be fun
to be the sky
and see an eagle
soaring high,
or hear and see
a gleaming jet
climb higher, higher,
higher yet.

But best of all,
the sky can trace
the route of rockets
out in space.
When eagles, jets
and rockets fly,
it must be fun
to be the sky.

Laughing Tomatoes

by Francisco X. Alarcón

in our backyard
we plant
tomatoes

the happiest
of all
vegetables

with joy
they grow round
with flavor

laughing
they change
to red

turning
their wire-framed
bushes

into
Christmas trees
in spring

Fishes' Evening Song

by Dahlov Ipcar

Flip flop,
Flip flap,
Slip slap,
Lip lap;
Water sounds,
Soothing sounds.
We fan our fins
As we lie
Resting here
Eye to eye.
Water falls
Drop by drop,
Plip plop,
Drip drop,
Plink plunk,
Splash splish;
Fish fins fan,
Fish tails swish,
Swush, swash, swish.
This we wish . . .
Water cold,
Water clear,
Water smooth,
Just to soothe
Sleepy fish.

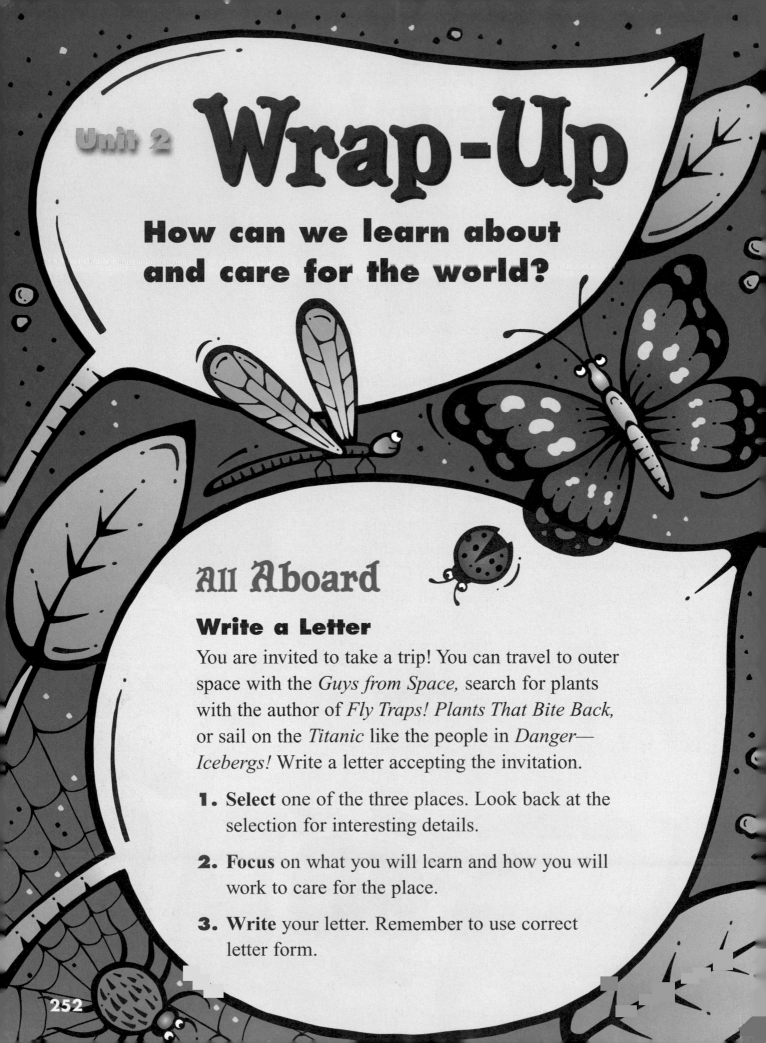

Wrap-Up

How can we learn about and care for the world?

All Aboard

Write a Letter

You are invited to take a trip! You can travel to outer space with the *Guys from Space,* search for plants with the author of *Fly Traps! Plants That Bite Back,* or sail on the *Titanic* like the people in *Danger—Icebergs!* Write a letter accepting the invitation.

1. **Select** one of the three places. Look back at the selection for interesting details.

2. **Focus** on what you will learn and how you will work to care for the place.

3. **Write** your letter. Remember to use correct letter form.

Special Alert

Deliver a News Report

Work with a partner to deliver a TV news report on fire, storm, hurricane, or tornado safety tips. Look back at *Tornado Alert* for information.

1. **Select** a topic for your safety tip report.

2. **Skim** *Tornado Alert* to decide on the kinds of tips you want to include. Practice what you will say.

3. **Report** your tips to the class. Make a small tip sheet for each classmate to keep.

Round Robin

Retell a Selection

In round-robin storytelling, each person takes a turn telling a part of a story. Work with a group of classmates to retell one of the selections you have read in Unit 2.

1. **Choose** a selection. Decide who will tell each part.

2. **Practice** retelling in round-robin style.

3. **When** your group is ready, **retell** the selection to others.

Describe Without Words

Create Art

Nights of the Pufflings tells many facts about puffins and pufflings. You see the birds in the daytime and at night, on land and on sea. Which part was your favorite? How would you show it without using words?

1. **Look back** at the selection. Think about your favorite part.

2. **Draw** a picture, make a diorama, or create another art project to show it.

3. **Present** your creation to the class. Let others guess which part of the selection your artwork shows.

Test Talk

Understand the Question

Find Key Words in the Text

Before you can answer a test question, you have to know where to look for the answer. A test on "Myths About Tornadoes," pages 206–207, might have this question.

Test Question 1

What does the word *myth* mean in this article? Use details from the article to support your answer.

Make sure that you understand the question.

Find the key words. Finish the statement "I need to find out . . ."

Decide where you will look for the answer.

- Some test questions tell you to look in one place in the text. The answer is *right there*.

- Other test questions tell you to look for information that is in different parts of the selection. You have to *think and search*.

- Still other test questions tell you to combine what *you* know with what the *author* tells you. The answer comes from the *author and you*.

See how one student figures out where to look for the answer.

Myth . . . I see the heading **Myth** many times in this article. So, I'll have to think and search for the answer.

I see that the headings **Myth** and **Truth** always go together. So they must be related. The first myth says you should try to outrun a tornado in your car. The first truth says you should seek shelter instead. So, a **myth** must be something that people think is true, but isn't. I'll read the other myths and truths to see if I'm right.

Try it!

Now use what you learned to figure out where to look for the answer to these test questions on "Myths About Tornadoes," pages 206–207.

Test Question 2

What amazing occurrence happened after horses were lifted up in a tornado? Use details from the article to explain your answer.

Test Question 3

Why did the author include a section called "Facts About Tornadoes"?

Ⓐ to give readers more information

Ⓑ to entertain readers

Ⓒ to show readers how much the author knows

Ⓓ to tell readers how the author feels

Getting the Job Done

How can we learn from everything we do?

Steps in a Process

- Following **steps in a process** usually means doing or making something.

- A process is a number of steps that follow in a certain order, from start to finish.

- Sometimes the steps in a process are shown in pictures as well as words.

Read "Cartoon Drawing" from *Cartooning for Kids* **by Carol Lea Benjamin.**

Write About It

1. Follow the steps given for drawing the pig. Share your drawing with a classmate.

2. Were the steps easy to follow? Why or why not?

Cartoon Drawing
by Carol Lea Benjamin

Get some paper and a pencil. You're going to begin by drawing a circle. Don't worry if the circle isn't perfectly round or if the beginning and the end of the circle don't meet. It doesn't matter. Don't jump ahead and try to copy the finished character. Even if the steps look easy to you, you're more likely to draw the character well if you go step by step.

1. Draw a circle.

2. Draw a smaller oval in the lower half of the circle.

3. Two little vertical lines in the oval become nostrils. Dots would work just as well.

4. Draw two small triangles for ears.

5. Two small vertical lines become eyes. Now your drawing will look like this.

6. Short horizontal lines look like eyebrows.

7. This character needs a mouth. It's just a small curve.

8. Hey! That's upside down.

9. Ah. Good work, cartoonist! Give your pig a name and . . .

10. Some lunch.

In *What Do Authors Do?*, follow the steps an author takes to write a story.

259

Vocabulary

Words to Know

suggestions libraries museums
information difficult authors

Many words have more than one
meaning. To decide which meaning of
a word is correct, look for clues in a
nearby sentence or paragraph.

Read this paragraph. Pay special
attention to its meaning as a whole.
Decide whether *difficult* means "not
easy to please" or "hard to do."

Writers' Work

Lee and Jae are authors who write children's
books. It is difficult for them to write a book
about Egypt because they don't know much
about it. They need more information about
mummies. They visit several libraries to find out
more. One librarian gives them suggestions of
books to read. Lee and Jae visit museums too.
After looking at displays, they are ready to write.

Write About It

What is the best way to find
information for a report? Use some
vocabulary words to make a tip list.

What Do Authors Do?

written and illustrated by Eileen Christelow

Authors get ideas for books at the strangest moments!

263

When authors have ideas for books, they start to write.

Sometimes it is difficult to find the words.

Some authors write notes about what might happen in the story. They make lists or outlines.

Some authors who write picture books are also illustrators. Sometimes they sketch as they write. The sketches give them ideas.

Sometimes authors need more information.

So they go to libraries, historical societies, museums. . . .

They read books, old newspapers, magazines, letters,
and diaries written long ago. They take notes.

They interview people. They take more notes.

They listen and watch.

They write and write and write . . .

and cross things out . . .

throw parts of the story away . . . and start again.

Sometimes authors read their stories to their families. Their families make suggestions.

Sometimes they read to author friends in a writers' group.
The friends make suggestions.

Sometimes authors get stuck, so they put their books away for a while.

But usually, when they are doing something else, they get unstuck.

Then they start to write again.

Authors who are also illustrators make
a dummy of the book to show how it will
look with illustrations.

It can take one year, two years, or more to finish
writing a manuscript! When the stories are finished,
authors send their manuscripts to publishers.

Sometimes they wait for weeks or months to hear
whether the publishers like their books.

Most authors have received rejection letters.
Some rejection letters are encouraging. Some are not.

But authors are very persistent people. They work on their
manuscripts some more. They send their manuscripts out
to other publishers.

Authors are very pleased when they find a publisher!

About the Author/Illustrator

Hi! I'm Eileen Christelow.

Books have always been important to Eileen Christelow. Even before she could read, she loved them. "When I was about three or four, I dreamed I could read," she remembers, "turning page after page and reading all the words. But when I woke up, I could no longer read." When she did learn to read, she spent a lot of her time doing what she had dreamed.

Ms. Christelow got her love of books from her parents. Her father liked to read books about things such as economics and history, but he also loved comic books. Ms. Christelow and her brother were allowed to see the comic books only after their father finished them.

Later, when Ms. Christelow had a child of her own, they went to the library each week. Ms. Christelow began to think that maybe she could create a children's book. She found out that sometimes doing the writing and the illustrating is not as easy as it looks. Like the authors in *What Do Authors Do?*, it took her a long time to get her first picture book just right.

Reader Response

Open for Discussion

Both authors saw the same thing happen and got different story ideas. If you saw what they saw, what would your story be about? Why?

Comprehension Check

1. Why do you think Eileen Christelow tells about two authors in her story? Look back through the story for details to explain your answer.

2. In this selection, what do the authors do when they are stuck? Which author do you think has the better way of getting unstuck? Use details to explain.

3. How do you think an author feels when a book is rejected? Look back at the story for details to support your answer.

4. According to *What Do Authors Do?*, what is the very first **step in the process** of writing a book? (Steps in a Process)

5. What is the **step in the process** that comes right after research? (Steps in a Process)

Test Prep

Look Back and Write

Look back on pages 272–273. Why is it a good idea to read your story aloud? Use details from the text to support your answer.

Science Connection

How to Read an Informational Article

1. Preview

- This informational article has many parts. Most parts have headings. Which part tells you the topic of the article? What will you find out in the other parts?

2. Read and Use a Chart

- Read the article to find out about animal senses. As you read, use a chart to take notes. Write the most important ideas under the headings *Touch*, *Sight*, *Hearing*, *Smell*, and *Taste*.

3. Think and Connect

Think about *What Do Authors Do?* Then look over your notes from "Super Senses."

Imagine you are an author from *What Do Authors Do?* Use the information from your chart to write a new chapter in your story about Rufus and Max.

SUPER SENSES

BY TINA ADLER

Walking through town, a person hears a noisy bus, feels the sun's heat, smells and tastes a vendor's pretzel, and sees a friend approaching—using all five senses. All animals have similar senses, but most have developed a particularly keen sense or two to match their specific survival needs. Moles, which live in darkness underground, have little use for good eyesight. They rely instead on a well-developed sense of touch to find food. Above ground, a jumping spider's exceptional sense is sight.

What's your strongest sense? Check out some super senses in the animal kingdom on these pages and see how you compare.

Echo Echo

The ears on a leaf-nosed bat tower over its head. Bats rely on their hearing to navigate in the dark. They make high-pitched clicks and cries that humans can't hear, then listen for the echo that sounds when the noises bounce off nearby objects.

TOUCH

Animals that are active at night tend to have a particularly well-developed sense of touch. So do animals that live underground. Often more useful to them than eyesight, the sense of touch gives animals information about their surroundings. Animals also use touching and feeling to communicate or to find food. Touch receptors are often concentrated around body parts such as whiskers.

By a Whisker

A cat's whiskers act as very sensitive feelers. These special hairs stick out from the cat's cheeks, chin, and above its eyes. A cat tends to be most active at night. Whiskers help it feel its way around in the dark.

SIGHT

Birds of prey have the best distance vision in the animal kingdom. Nocturnal creatures, or animals that are active at night, have the best night vision. To see, eyes collect available light and focus it onto receptors, which send signals to the brain. The brain interprets the signals, and then an animal knows what it is seeing.

Eagle Eyes

A bald eagle (above) can spot a mouse in a field from thousands of feet high in the sky. An eagle's keen eyesight also allows it to focus on objects in front of it or to either side without moving its head. Eagle eyesight is four times as sharp as that of a person with perfect vision.

Multivision

A honeybee (below) has five eyes—three small eyes on the top of its head and one large eye on each side of its head. Bees can see light rays and flower markings that are invisible to humans. Their vision helps the insects zero in on flowers that have pollen to gather.

HEARING

When an animal hears something, it's because sound waves make its eardrums vibrate, which send signals to the brain. Animals that hunt by sound have remarkable hearing. They listen for faint rustling of moving prey. Bats and whales find their way around by listening to sounds bounce off objects. Still other animals listen for sounds from their own species to find one another.

Whale Wails

A humpback whale communicates with beeps and calls that sound like songs. A whale miles away can hear the song. Male humpbacks repeat long songs that probably attract females and warn other males away.

SMELL & TASTE

Some animals can smell a variety of odors really well, while others specialize. A male silkworm moth can sniff out a potential mate seven miles away, but he smells nothing else. Eels' sense of smell is so well-developed that they can detect a thimbleful of an artificial scent diluted in a huge lake. Smell and taste often work together. As a test, hold your nose as you take a bite of food. It probably won't taste as flavorful as usual.

Nose Knows

A bloodhound's ability to smell helps people. Frequently used for tracking lost children and escaped prisoners, bloodhounds can follow a scent that is nearly four days old. The membrane in a bloodhound's nose that detects odors is fifty times bigger and a million times more sensitive than a human's.

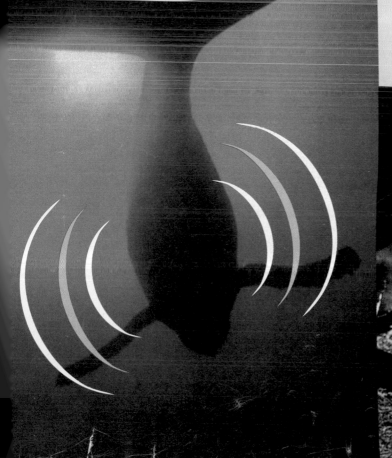

Skill Lesson

Summarizing

- In a **summary** a few sentences tell the main ideas in a story or article.

- A summary of a story tells what the story is about without telling details.

Read "To Catch a Rabbit" from *The Blue Hill Meadows* by Cynthia Rylant.

Talk About It

1. Is **a.** or **b.** a better summary of the story?

   a. Willie's mother enjoyed seeing wild rabbits. To surprise her, Willie planted a small garden to bring rabbits where his mother could see them.

   b. On Mother's Day, Willie's mother saw him on the ground by her cherry tree. He was planting seeds and putting signs to mark the places.

2. What reasons do you have for your choice?

To Catch a Rabbit

by Cynthia Rylant

Wild rabbits are not easy to catch. They want to be free and they use their wits to stay that way. But Willie wasn't interested in catching the rabbit. His mother would not want a rabbit in a cage.

Willie was interested in making the rabbit stay, in making Eva's cherry tree the most wonderful place in the world for a rabbit to be.

And Willie thought he knew how to do it.

So, when Mother's Day morning came, Eva Meadow rose early from bed as usual, put on her robe, and quietly padded into the kitchen to

start Sunday coffee brewing. And as always, she glanced out the window to see if the wild rabbit had come back to the cherry tree. She hoped to see that lovely sight again.

But this morning what Eva Meadow saw was a far lovelier sight than a wild brown rabbit. She saw her own boy Willie kneeling beneath that tree, trowel in hand, pouring seeds into the earth he had overturned. All around him in a circle were little signs marking those seeds he had already planted: ALFALFA, CARROTS, RADISHES, LETTUCE.

Eva pushed open the screen door. Willie smiled. "Happy Mother's Day, Mom."

CARROT SEED

LOOK AHEAD

In *Tops and Bottoms*, Hare tricks Bear into sharing his food. Read and think about how it could be summarized.

Vocabulary

Words to Know

business   cheated partners
harvesting clever   wealth
lazy

Words with opposite meanings, like
up and *down,* are **antonyms.** You can
often figure out the meaning of a word
by finding a clue near it. Sometimes
this clue is an antonym.

Read this paragraph. Notice how the
antonym *hardworking* helps you
understand what *lazy* means.

The Lazy Cricket

Two crickets were <u>partners</u>. They had a
<u>business</u> together <u>harvesting</u> wheat. One cricket
was hardworking. The other was <u>lazy</u> but <u>clever</u>.
Every night, the crickets piled up the wheat they
had harvested. The lazy cricket <u>cheated</u> his
partner out of his <u>wealth</u> by switching piles of
wheat. One day . . .

Talk About It

Finish the story. Tell how the
lazy cricket learns a lesson.
Use some vocabulary words.

Tops and Bottoms

and Bottoms

adapted and illustrated
by Janet Stevens

ONCE upon a time there lived a
very lazy bear who had lots of money
and lots of land. His father had been
a hard worker and a smart business
bear, and he had given all of his
wealth to his son.

But all Bear wanted to do was sleep.

Not far down the road lived a hare. Although Hare was clever, he sometimes got into trouble. He had once owned land, too, but now he had nothing. He had lost a risky bet with a tortoise and had sold all of his land to Bear to pay off the debt.

Hare and his family were in very bad shape.

"The children are so hungry, Father Hare! We must think of something!" Mrs. Hare cried one day. So Hare and Mrs. Hare put their heads together and cooked up a plan.

The next day Hare hopped down the road to Bear's house. Bear, of course, was asleep.

"Hello, Bear, wake up! It's your neighbor, Hare, and I have an idea!"

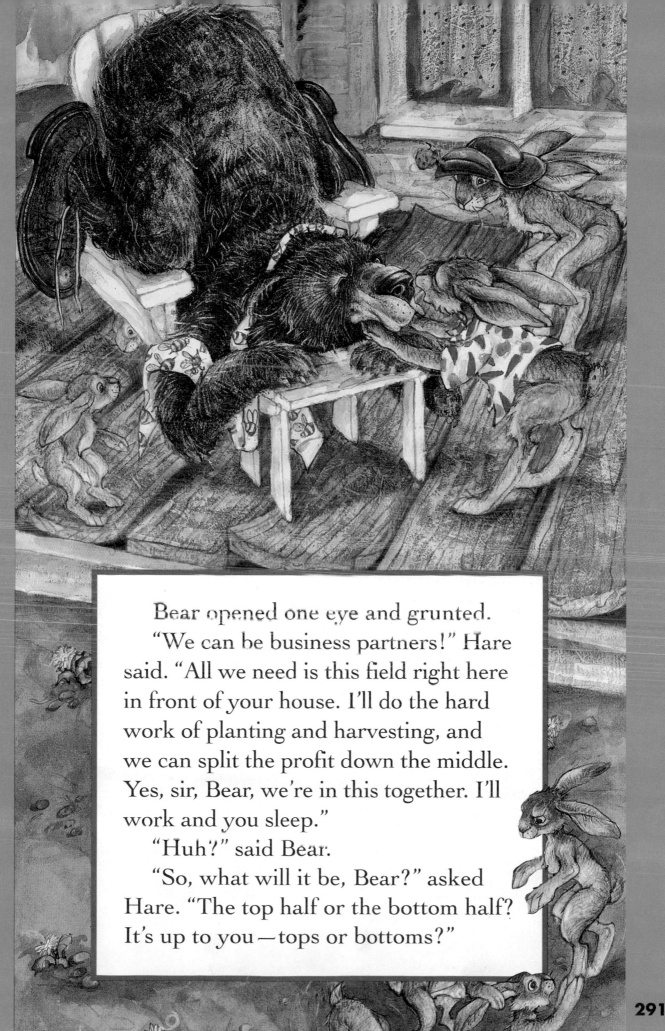

Bear opened one eye and grunted.

"We can be business partners!" Hare said. "All we need is this field right here in front of your house. I'll do the hard work of planting and harvesting, and we can split the profit down the middle. Yes, sir, Bear, we're in this together. I'll work and you sleep."

"Huh?" said Bear.

"So, what will it be, Bear?" asked Hare. "The top half or the bottom half? It's up to you—tops or bottoms?"

"Uh, let's see," Bear said with a yawn. "I'll take the top half, Hare. Right—tops."

Hare smiled. "It's a done deal, Bear."

So Bear went back to sleep, and Hare and his family went to work. Hare planted, Mrs. Hare watered, and everyone weeded.

Bear slept as the crops grew.

When it was time for the harvest, Hare called out, "Wake up, Bear! You get the tops and I get the bottoms."

Hare and his family dug up the carrots, the radishes, and the beets. Hare plucked off all the tops, tossed them into a pile for Bear, and put the bottoms aside for himself.

Bear stared at his pile. "But, Hare, all the best parts are in your half!"

"You chose the tops, Bear," Hare said.

"Now, Hare, you've tricked me. You plant this field again—and this season I want the bottoms!"

Hare agreed. "It's a done deal, Bear."

So Bear went back to sleep, and
Hare and his family went to work.
They planted, watered, and weeded.

Bear slept as the crops grew.

When it was time for the harvest, Hare called out, "Wake up, Bear! You get the bottoms and I get the tops."

Hare and his family gathered up the lettuce, the broccoli, and the celery. Hare pulled off the bottoms for Bear and put the tops in his own pile.

Bear looked at his pile and scowled. "Hare, you have cheated me again."

"But, Bear," Hare said, "you wanted the bottoms this time."

Bear growled. "You plant this field again, Hare. You've tricked me twice, and you owe me one season of both tops and bottoms!"

"You're right, poor old Bear," sighed Hare. "It's only fair that you get both tops and bottoms this time. It's a done deal, Bear."

So Bear went back to sleep, and Hare and his family went to work. They planted, watered, and weeded, then watered and weeded some more.

Bear slept as the crops grew.

When it was time for the harvest, Hare called out, "Wake up, Bear! This time you get the tops and the bottoms!"

There in front of Bear's house lay a high field of corn. Hare and his family yanked up every cornstalk. Hare tugged off the roots at the bottom and the tassels at the top and put them in a pile for Bear. Then he carefully collected the ears of corn in the middle and placed them in his own pile.

Bear rubbed his eyes and watched. "See, Bear? You get the tops and the bottoms. I get the middles. Yes, sir, Bear. It's a done deal!"

By now Bear was wide awake. "That's it, Hare!" he hollered. "From now on, I'll plant my own crops and take the tops, bottoms, and middles!"

Hare and his family scooped up the corn and hopped down the road toward home.

Bear never again slept through
a season of planting and harvesting.
Hare bought back his land with the
profit from the crops, and he and Mrs.
Hare opened a vegetable stand.

And although Hare and Bear learned to live happily as neighbors, they never became business partners again!

From the Author
Janet Stevens

I was poking around in the library one day, looking for book ideas, but I wasn't having much luck on my own. Judy Volc, the children's librarian, seems to know everything about what kids like to read, so I asked her, "Do you have any suggestions? What stories do kids like?" She immediately replied, "*Tops and Bottoms!* Kids love that story—they ask for it over and over, and you could make it into a super picture book."

So began the *Tops and Bottoms* adventure. The librarian gave me several versions of the story, and I set out to retell it in my own words. But those words didn't come easily. The more I tried, the worse it sounded. So I put the words away. I thought, "I'll just draw! I'll have some fun." And so I began drawing *Tops and Bottoms* without a written story of my own.

Most of the versions the librarian gave me had people as the main characters. I like to draw animals, so I decided to make the lazy character a bear. But who should be his partner? First I tried a bear with a prairie dog.

Then I tried a bear with a fox. That wasn't right either. Then I changed the bear to a turtle. That switch reminded me of my illustrations of *The Hare and the Tortoise*, in which the hare loses the race. A loss like that could be the reason that Hare doesn't have any money! So I returned to my first idea of Bear, and his business partner became Hare! Sometimes you have to try lots of ideas before you get one that feels just right.

One of the most puzzling things to me about *Tops and Bottoms* is how I convinced myself I couldn't write the story. We really can talk ourselves into—or out of—things. It's sort of like *The Little Engine That Could;* the little train doesn't say, "I think I can't, I think I can't!" Drawing pictures first of Bear and Hare helped me get to know them. As I dressed them up and knew their personalities, they started to talk. Then I could write the story. The more I drew them the more confident I became. The words flowed easily once I quit worrying about whether I could write. That's why I dedicated the book to Judy Volc, the children's librarian; she thought I could create a *Tops and Bottoms* picture book from the beginning. All I needed to do was convince myself!

Reader Response

Open for Discussion

How do the pictures help tell the story? Tell which picture is your favorite, and why.

Comprehension Check

1. Does Hare treat Bear fairly? Why do you think this? Use details from the story to support your answer.

2. Look back on pages 289–290. Tell one or two words that describe Hare's character.

3. Look back at the story. Make a chart that lists vegetables in the story by the part that we eat—tops, bottoms, or middles. Add other vegetables that you eat.

4. To make a **summary** of the story, answer these questions. (Summary)
   - What does Hare want?
   - How does he try to get it?
   - Does Hare get what he wants?

5. To make a different **summary** of the story, answer these questions.(Summary)
   - What does Bear want?
   - How does he try to get it?
   - Does Bear get what he wants?

Test Prep

Look Back and Write

Look back at pages 291–302. Tell what happens from the time Hare and Bear agree to be business partners up to the time Bear decides to plant his own crops. Use the text and pictures to support your answer.

Food from Plants

by David Burnie

PLANTS HAVE BEEN GROWN as food crops for thousands of years. The earliest humans lived in groups that roamed the countryside in search of food. Eventually these peoples settled down and began to grow their own food. When the time came to gather seeds to produce crops for the following year, they took seeds from the healthiest plants. As they did this year after year, they began to produce better crop plants. As people began to farm in different parts of the world, different crops were grown in each place. This meant that when early travelers first visited distant places, they found many new and exciting foods to bring home. The crops we eat today come from many different parts of the world.

Wild chicory

Primitive form of corn plant and cob

Modern corncob

KEPT IN THE DARK
Chicory is grown in the dark so it will not be bitter.

Farmed chicory shoot

PRIMITIVE CORN
Corn is a cereal grain. Like wheat and rice it is a member of the grass family. It was first grown in the Americas, and some primitive forms of corn can still be found there. The size and shape of the modern corncob have been increased.

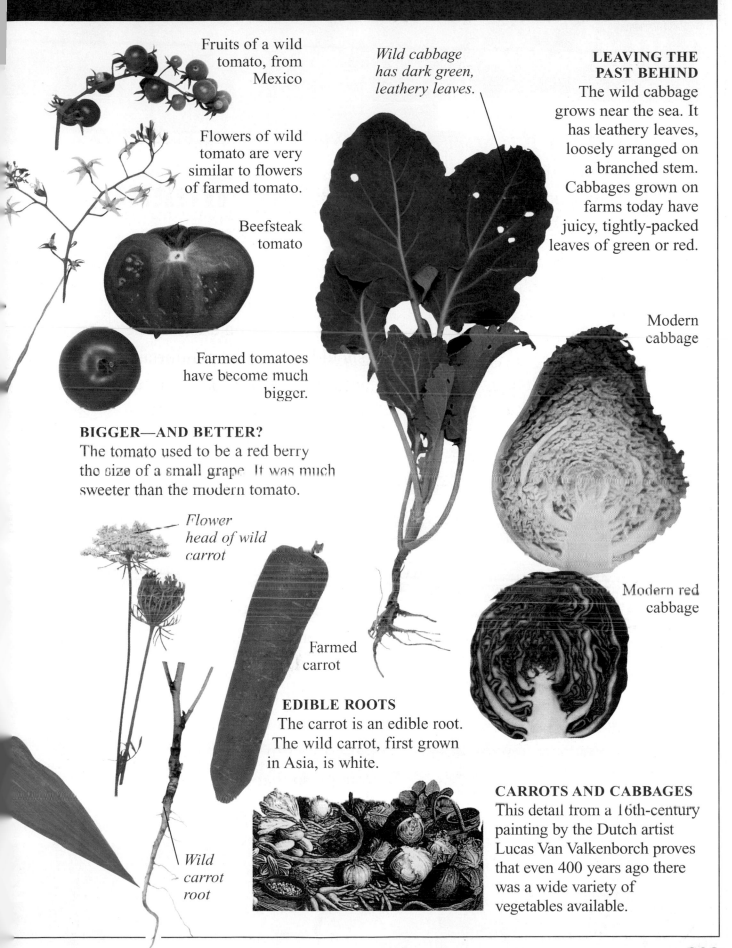

Fruits of a wild tomato, from Mexico

Flowers of wild tomato are very similar to flowers of farmed tomato.

Beefsteak tomato

Farmed tomatoes have become much bigger.

BIGGER—AND BETTER?
The tomato used to be a red berry the size of a small grape. It was much sweeter than the modern tomato.

Flower head of wild carrot

Farmed carrot

EDIBLE ROOTS
The carrot is an edible root. The wild carrot, first grown in Asia, is white.

Wild carrot root

Wild cabbage has dark green, leathery leaves.

LEAVING THE PAST BEHIND
The wild cabbage grows near the sea. It has leathery leaves, loosely arranged on a branched stem. Cabbages grown on farms today have juicy, tightly-packed leaves of green or red.

Modern cabbage

Modern red cabbage

CARROTS AND CABBAGES
This detail from a 16th-century painting by the Dutch artist Lucas Van Valkenborch proves that even 400 years ago there was a wide variety of vegetables available.

Skill Lesson

Text Structure

- **Text structure** is the way a story or article is organized.

- One way an author can organize the text is to tell things in the order that they happen.

- Use what you already know about story order to understand what you are reading.

Read "Puppy Training" from *Puppy Training and Critters, Too!* by Judy Petersen-Fleming and Bill Fleming.

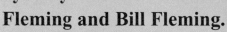

Talk About It

1. How is this article organized?

2. What events happen once the puppy is used to wearing the collar?

Puppy Training

by Judy Petersen-Fleming
and Bill Fleming

Before you start training your puppy to walk on a leash, she should already be comfortable wearing a collar. Once she's used to her collar, you can make wearing a leash comfortable and positive. Start by putting on the leash and holding the other end so that it's loose. *Never* hold the leash tight so that you're pulling on your puppy. Run around and play with your puppy until she feels comfortable wearing the leash.

Now that your puppy is content *wearing* a leash, it is time to teach her to *walk* on a leash. It is important to teach this to your puppy so that she will be able to

accompany you away from home. Start by holding the end of the leash with your right hand and the middle of the leash with your left hand. Your puppy should *always* be on your left side. Start walking slowly with your puppy next to you. If she stops, say "Heel" and tug gently on the leash. This will teach your puppy to walk beside you. Remember to keep these sessions short. Make walking on a leash fun for your puppy by taking her to new places each time.

LOOK AHEAD

In *Mom's Best Friend,* a woman has to learn how to train her new dog. As you read, think about how the selection is organized.

Vocabulary

Words to Know

bounded	easily	introduce
correcting	guide	patient
direction	harness	

Words that are pronounced and spelled the same but have different meanings are called **homonyms.** *Bark* (on a tree) and *bark* (like a dog) are homonyms. To know the meaning being used, look for clues in the sentences near it.

Read this paragraph. Decide if the homonym *bounded* means "limited" or "jumped."

Harley Comes Home

The trainer came to <u>introduce</u> me to Harley, my new dog. Harley <u>bounded</u> in, excited to be home. I learned to hold his <u>harness</u>. Harley would <u>guide</u> me in the right <u>direction</u>. He <u>easily</u> helped me around the house, but he needed <u>correcting</u> when we went outside. I'll be <u>patient</u>—Harley will learn soon enough!

Write About It

Use vocabulary words to write ways that animals help people.

MOM's
Best Friend

by Sally Hobart Alexander   photographs by George Ancona

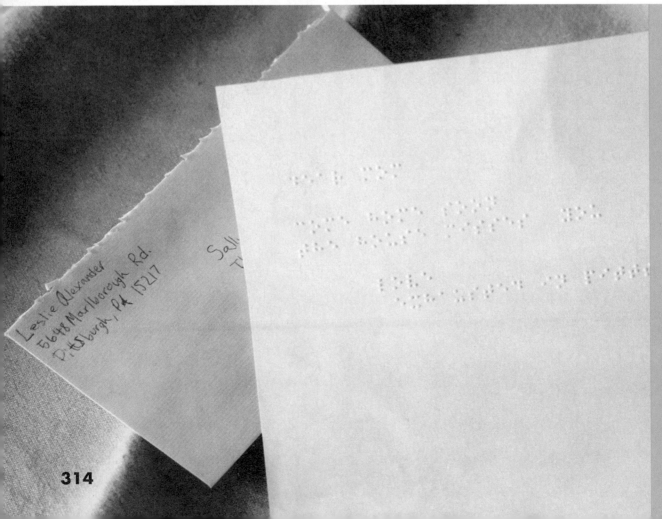

Leslie Alexander
5648 Marlborough Rd.
Pittsburgh, PA 15217

Sall

The whole family loved Marit, Mom's dog guide. But when Marit dies, Mom has to go away to Seeing Eye, a school where new dog guides and their owners are trained. Leslie, Joel, and Dad are having trouble taking care of things without Mom.

Dear Mom,
Come home soon. The house misses you.
Love,
Exhausted in Pittsburgh

Mom wrote back.

Dear Exhausted,

Hang on. We'll be home to "hound" you Thursday. Be prepared. When you see me, I will have grown four more feet.

Mom

I couldn't laugh. I was too tired and worried. What if I couldn't love Ursula? Marit was the best dog ever.

Soon they arrived. Ursula yanked at her leash and sprang up on me. She pawed my shoulders, stomach, and arms just the way Marit used to, nearly knocking me over. She leaped onto Joel, licking him all over. As she bounded up onto me again, I realized Mom was right. Like magic, I was crazy about this shrimpy new dog.

But by the end of the day, I had a new worry. Was *Ursula* going to love *me?* She seemed friendly enough, but keyed up, even lost in our house.

"Remember how Marit loved you, Leslie? When you were little, she let you stand on her back to see out the window. Ursula will be just nuts about you. Love is the whole reason this dog guide business works."

So I tried to be patient and watched Mom work hard. First she showed one route in our neighborhood to Ursula and walked it over and over. Then she taught her a new route, repeated that, and reviewed the old one. Every day she took Ursula on two trips, walking two or three miles. She fed her, groomed her, gave her obedience training. Twice a week Mom cleaned Ursula's ears and brushed her teeth.

"I'm as busy as I was when you and Joel were little!" she said.

Mom and Ursula played for forty-five minutes each day. Joel, Dad, and I were only allowed to watch. Ursula needed to form her biggest attachment to Mom.

Mom made Ursula her shadow. When she showered or slept, Ursula was right there.

till, Ursula didn't eat well—only half the amount she'd been eating at Seeing Eye. And she tested Mom, pulling her into branches, stepping off curbs. Once she tried to take a shortcut home. Another time, because she was nervous, she crossed a new street diagonally.

Crossing streets is tricky. Ursula doesn't know when the light is green. Mom knows. If she hears the cars moving beside her in the direction in which she's walking, the light is green. If they're moving right and left in front of her, it's red.

Mom said it takes four to six months for the dogs to settle down. But no matter how long she and Ursula are teamed up together, Ursula will need some correcting. For instance, Ursula might act so cute that a passerby will reach out to pet her. Then Mom will have to scold Ursula and ask the person not to pet a dog guide. If people give Ursula attention while she's working, she forgets to do her job.

After a month at home, Ursula emptied her food bowl every time. She knew all the routes, and Mom could zip around as easily as she had with Marit.

"Now it's time to start the loneliness training," Mom said. She left Ursula alone in the house, at first for a short time while she went jogging with Dad. Ursula will never be able to take Mom jogging because she can't guide at high speeds.

ach week Mom increased the amount of time Ursula was alone. I felt sorry for our pooch, but she did well: no barking, no chewing on furniture.

Then Mom said Joel and I could introduce Ursula to our friends, one at a time. They could pet her when she was out of harness.

Every morning Ursula woke Joel and me. Every night she sneaked into my bed for a snooze.

Finally Mom allowed Joel and me to play with Ursula, and I knew: shrimpy little Ursula had fallen for us, and we were even crazier about her.

But we haven't forgotten Marit. Joel says that Ursula is the best dog alive. And I always say she's the best dog in this world.

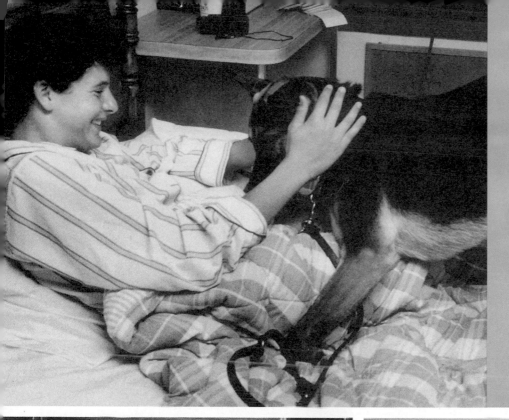

Sally Hobart Alexander

When it comes to writing stories, Sally Hobart Alexander would like everyone to know this: "If I can do it, you can too!" Ms. Alexander started telling stories to her first child. By the time her second child came along, she could invent a story within seconds, using whatever characters her children suggested.

Ms. Alexander's stories for her children were make believe. Her book *Mom's Best Friend* and an earlier story, *Mom Can't See Me,* are based on her real-life experiences with blindness.

George Ancona

When he was young, George Ancona's father took him to see huge ships on the waterfront in Brooklyn, New York. "It's like seeing something awe-inspiring and you just have to say, 'WOW',," he remembers. He thinks about that feeling as he creates his books.

Mr. Ancona has taken photographs for books written by other people as well as for his own books. For each book he took the pictures first. "The words came later," he says. "They filled in what the pictures couldn't convey."

Reader Response

Open for Discussion

Why is a dog Mom's best friend? When might an animal be your best friend?

Comprehension Check

1. Look back at page 316. In her reply to Leslie's letter, Mom makes two funny word jokes. Explain one of them. Use the text to help you.

2. Why is a dog guide's training so important? Use the text to support your answer.

3. Look back at pages 316–319. Why is Leslie worried about whether Ursula will love her?

4. *Mom's Best Friend* is nonfiction, but its **text structure** is like a story. How are most stories told? (Text Structure)

5. Think about the **text structure** of this selection. What important event happened before the selection began? (Text Structure)

Test Prep

Look Back and Write

Look back at pages 315–322. Why do you think the author wrote about her dog guide? Was she trying to inform, to entertain, to express or describe, or to persuade you about dog guides? Use details to support your answer.

325

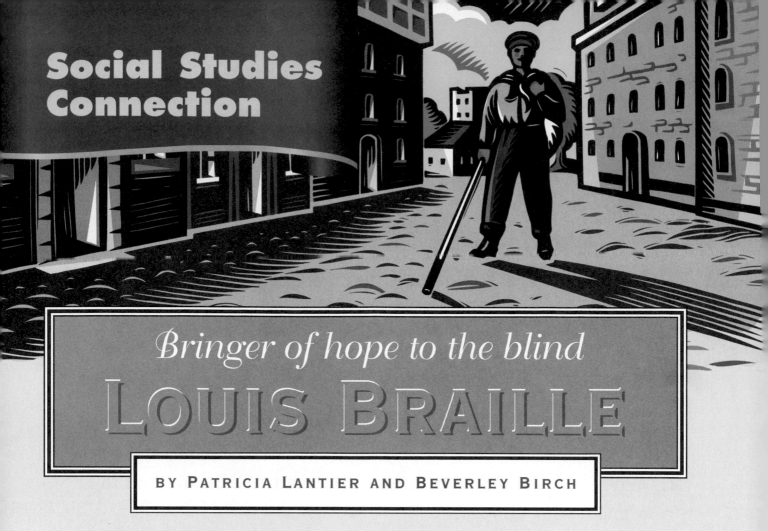

Bringer of hope to the blind

LOUIS BRAILLE

BY PATRICIA LANTIER AND BEVERLEY BIRCH

LOUIS'S QUEST

The dark room was very quiet. The only sounds were the creaking of iron beds, the rustling of blankets, the breathing of sleeping boys, and a low, knocking noise.

One boy was still awake. He sat upright in a bed balancing a small board with papers on it across his knees. The boy pressed down on a piece of paper with a pointed instrument and made short, punching sounds.

It did not matter if the damp, cold room was dark. The boy could not see the dark. He could not see anything around the room. He could not even see the board across his knees.

The boy was blind. He had been blind for a long time. And all the other boys in the room with him were also blind.

The boy was very tired, but he did not let himself fall asleep. He kept punching the paper with his pointed instrument. He listened closely to the measured sounds of his movements.

Fourteen-year-old Louis Braille spent many nights awake with his board and paper. He often worked until the new day began. Then it was time for lessons, and he had no more free time.

special school in Paris. He knew, however, that there must be a way for blind people to read and write easily. There had to be a way for them to share all there was to learn in the world.

Louis Braille believed that blind people did not have to be cut off from a normal life.

A DETERMINED CHILD

Louis had been working on this project for months. He had even taken it home during school vacation. There he worked outside in the warmth of the sun all summer. Passing villagers would say to each other: "Ah, there's young Louis at his pinpricks again!"

Louis *was* making little pinholes in his paper. They were very special pinpricks. These pinpricks would one day become the alphabet for blind people all over the world. With this system, blind people would be able to communicate better. They would not have to feel trapped in their darkness. But in Braille's time, people did not believe that blind people could do anything important.

Louis Braille did not know how successful his system of dots would become. After all, he was just a fourteen-year-old blind student in a

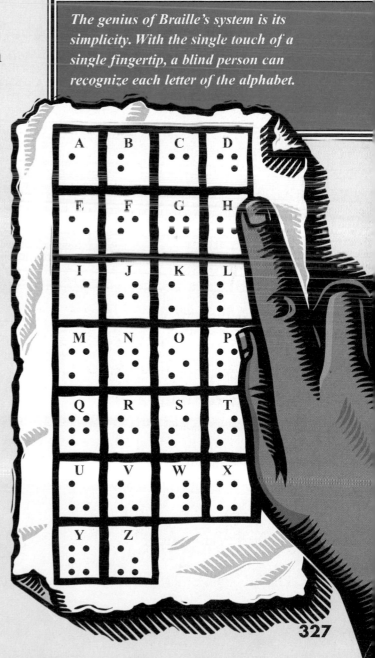

The genius of Braille's system is its simplicity. With the single touch of a single fingertip, a blind person can recognize each letter of the alphabet.

Skill Lesson

Visualizing

- To **visualize** is to create a picture in your mind.

- You can put yourself into the story or article by using all your senses when you read.

- When you read, use details in the text along with what you know about the subject to see, hear, smell, taste, and feel what the author describes.

Read "A Ride to the Stars" from *A Net of Stars* by Jennifer Richard Jacobson.

Write About It

1. What details in the first two paragraphs help you visualize the midway?

2. What details in the third and fourth paragraphs help you visualize what Etta sees, hears, and feels on the Ferris wheel?

A Ride to the Stars
by Jennifer Richard Jacobson

We always go back to the midway on the last night. Now the midway looks like a fairyland with rainbow lights. The carnival music sounds louder than the roller coaster screams.

"Stay together," says Daddy. Fiona and Harper pay fifty cents to try and win a prize.

I don't say anything. I run over to the woman in the booth and buy the right number of tickets. The ticket man takes my tickets and snaps the bar across my lap. I close my eyes tight tight, and feel the chair go up. I know I'm getting higher. I know I'm in the sky. When

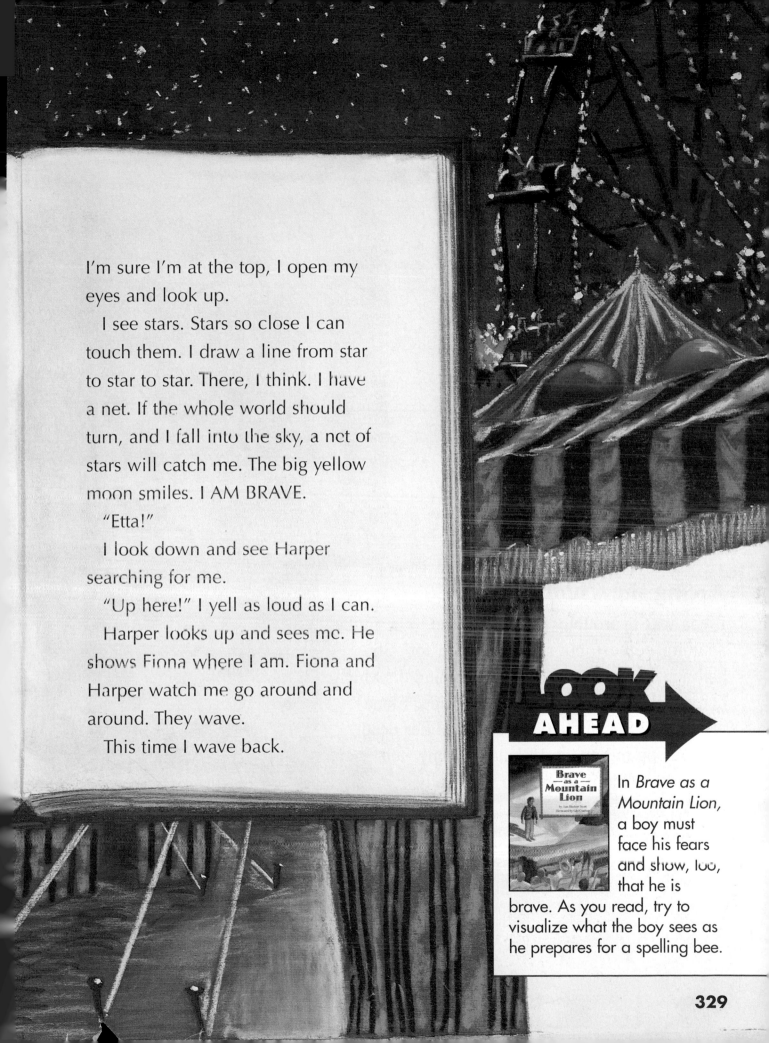

I'm sure I'm at the top, I open my eyes and look up.

I see stars. Stars so close I can touch them. I draw a line from star to star to star. There, I think. I have a net. If the whole world should turn, and I fall into the sky, a net of stars will catch me. The big yellow moon smiles. I AM BRAVE.

"Etta!"

I look down and see Harper searching for me.

"Up here!" I yell as loud as I can.

Harper looks up and sees me. He shows Fiona where I am. Fiona and Harper watch me go around and around. They wave.

This time I wave back.

LOOK AHEAD

In *Brave as a Mountain Lion*, a boy must face his fears and show, too, that he is brave. As you read, try to visualize what the boy sees as he prepares for a spelling bee.

Vocabulary

Words to Know

spelling	trouble	brave
afraid	reservation	silent

As you read, you may come across a word you don't know. To figure out its meaning, look for clues in the words and sentences around it. An explanation given before or after the unknown word may contain a clue to its meaning.

Notice how *reservation* is used in the paragraph below. Find an explanation near it.

Facing the Challenge

Elena was in trouble. She was proud to be in the spelling contest, but she was afraid too. She had never left the reservation, the land on which her people lived. On the long bus ride, Elena was silent. She spelled words out in her head. The bus pulled up, and Elena suddenly felt brave. She finally knew she was ready.

Write About It

Describe a time when you did something difficult. Use some vocabulary words.

Brave
— as a —
Mountain
Lion

by Ann Herbert Scott

illustrated by Glo Coalson

It was snowing hard. Pressing his face against the cold glass of the living room window, Spider could barely see his father's horses crowding against the fence. Soon the reservation would be covered with darkness.

Spider shivered. Any other night he would have been hoping his father would reach home before the snow drifted too high to push through. But tonight was different. Tonight he dreaded his father's coming.

In his pocket Spider could feel two pieces of paper from school. One he wanted to show his father. One he didn't. Not tonight. Not ever.

Beside him on the couch his sister Winona was playing with her doll. Lucky kid, thought Spider. Winona was too little to worry about anything, especially school.

Just then Spider saw the blinking red lights of the snowplow clearing the road beside their house. Right behind came his father's new blue pickup. Spider sighed. At least Dad was home safe. Now the trouble would begin!

Winona ran to the back door. But Spider stayed on the couch, waiting. From the kitchen he could smell dinner cooking. His favorite, deer meat. But tonight he didn't even feel like eating. Soon he heard the sound of his father and his brother Will stomping the snow from their boots.

Spider's father came in with an armful of mail from the post office. He hung up his hat and jacket on the pegs by the kitchen and stretched out in his favorite chair.

"So what did you do in school today?" he asked Spider.

"Not much," said Spider, feeling his pocket.

"Did you bring home any papers?"

Spider nodded. How did his father always know?

"Let's take a look," said his father.

Spider took the first paper from his pocket. "Here's the good one," he said.

"Spelling one hundred percent. Every word correct. Good for you, son."

"But, Dad, I'm in trouble." Spider shoved the other paper into his father's hand. "The teacher wants me to be in the big school spelling bee."

Spider's father read out loud: "Dear Parent, I am pleased to inform you that your son Spider has qualified for the school spelling bee, which will be held next Thursday night. We hope you and your family will attend."

Spider's mother and grandmother came in from the kitchen with the platter of deer meat and bowls of beans and corn for dinner. "That's a good report, Little Brother," his grandmother said, smiling.

"But I won't do it," said Spider.

"Why not?" asked Will.

"I'm too afraid," said Spider.

"But you're a brave boy," said his father. "Why are you afraid?"

"Dad," said Spider, "you have to stand high up on the stage in the gym and all the people look at you. I'm afraid my legs would freeze together and I wouldn't be able to walk. And if I did get up there, no sound would come out when I opened my mouth. It's too scary."

"Oh, I see," said his father.

Spider's mother put her hand on his shoulder. "You must be hungry. Let's eat."

After dinner, Spider sat by the wood stove doing his homework. "Dad, were you ever in a spelling bee?" he asked.

"As a matter of fact, I was."

"Were you scared?"

"I was very scared. I didn't even want do to it. But then my father told me to pretend I was a brave animal, the strongest, bravest animal I could think of. Then I wasn't afraid anymore."

Later, Spider sat up in bed thinking of animals who weren't afraid of anything. Above his head hung the picture of a mountain lion his dad had painted for him. How about a mountain lion, the King of the Beasts?

Spider took his flashlight from under his pillow and shined its beam on the face of the great wild creature. "Brave as a mountain lion," he said to himself in a loud, strong voice.

"Brave as a mountain lion," he repeated in his mind as he was falling asleep.

"I'll try to be brave as a mountain lion," he whispered to his father the next morning as he brushed his hair for school.

At recess the next day Spider peeked into the gymnasium. The huge room was empty. He looked up at the mural painting of the western Shoshone people of long ago. They were brave hunters of deer and antelope and elk, just as his father and his uncles were today.

At the far end of the gym was the scoreboard with the school's emblem, the eagle. Every Saturday in the winter Spider and his whole family came to cheer for Will and the basketball team. Those players weren't afraid of anything.

Then Spider stared up at the stage. That's where the spellers would stand. He could feel his throat tighten and hear his heart thumping, bumpity-bumpity-bumpity-bump. How could he ever get up there in front of all the people? Spider ran outside, slamming the gym door behind him.

That afternoon it was still snowing. At home Spider found his grandmother beading a hatband for his father's birthday. Spider watched her dip her needle into the bowls of red and black and white beads.

"Grandma, were you ever in a spelling bee?"

"No, I never was," his grandmother answered. "Are you thinking much about it?"

"All the time," said Spider.

"What's the worst part?"

"Being up on the stage with all the people looking at you."

"Oh, that's easy," said his grandmother. "You can be clever. Clever as a coyote. The coyote always has some trick to help him out of trouble. When you're up there on the stage, you don't have to look at the people. You can turn your back on them and pretend they aren't even there."

In bed that night Spider pulled the covers over his head. "Brave as a mountain lion, clever as a coyote," he kept repeating to himself as he fell asleep.

The next morning Spider scraped a peephole in the ice on his bedroom window. He couldn't see the far mountains for the swirling snow. He smiled as he packed his book bag. If it kept snowing like this, maybe the principal would close school tomorrow.

In class that day all everybody could talk about was the spelling bee. "Can we count on you, Spider?" asked Miss Phillips, his teacher.

Spider shook his head. "Maybe," he said. "I haven't made up my mind."

"You'd better make up your mind soon," said Miss Phillips. "The spelling bee is tomorrow night."

After lunch Spider walked by the gym door, but this time he didn't open it. He didn't have to. He remembered just how everything looked. Scary. When he thought about it, a shiver went all the way down his spine.

By the afternoon the snow had piled in drifts higher than Spider's head. Spider got a bowl of popcorn and went to the carport to watch Will shoot baskets. Time after time the ball slipped through the net. Will almost never missed.

"How about some popcorn for me?" Will asked his little brother. Spider brought back another bowl from the kitchen.

"Are you practicing for the spelling bee?" asked Will.

"I've decided not to be in it," said Spider. "I'm going to be brave when I'm bigger."

Will nodded. "I remember those spelling bees."

"Were you afraid?" asked Spider.

"I was scared silly," said Will. "Then I learned the secret."

"What's the secret?" asked Spider.

"To be silent."

"Silent?" asked Spider. "What does that do?"

"It keeps you cool. When I have a hard shot to make and the whole team depends on me, that's when I get very silent."

Spider didn't say anything. He just watched his
brother shooting one basket after another. Then he saw
her. High above the shelves of paint and livestock
medicines was a tiny insect. It was his old friend, Little
Spider, dangling on a long strand as she spun a new
part of her web. She was silent. Silent as the moon.

Spider laughed. How could he have forgotten!
Grandmother often told him how when he was a baby in
his cradle board he used to watch for hours while a little
spider spun her web above his head. She had been his
first friend. Ever since, his family had called him Spider.

Taking the stepladder, Spider climbed up close so
he could watch the tiny creature. How brave she was,
dropping down into space with nothing to hang onto.

And how clever, weaving a web out of nothing but her own secret self. "Say something," he whispered.

The little insect was silent. But Spider felt she was talking to him in her own mysterious way. "Listen to your spirit," she seemed to say. "Listen to your spirit and you'll never be afraid."

The next morning the snow had stopped. Outside Spider's window icicles glistened in the sun. No chance of school being closed today.

"Brave as a mountain lion, clever as a coyote, silent as a spider," Spider thought to himself as he buttoned his vest

Winona pushed open the door. "Are you going to do it?"

"I'm going to do it," Spider answered.

That night all the family came, his grandmother who lived with them and his other grandparents and his father and his mother and three aunts and two uncles and Will and Winona and lots of their cousins. Three of his cousins were going to be in the spelling bee too.

Brave as a mountain lion, Spider climbed up the steps to the stage. Clever as a coyote, he turned his back so he wouldn't see the rows of people down below. Silently, he listened to his spirit. Bumpity-bump-bump went his heart.

All the best spellers in his class were up there on the stage, standing in a line. The principal gave them the words, one by one.

At first the words were easy. "Yellow," said the principal. "I have a yellow dog."

Spider kept his eyes on the principal's face. "Yellow," said Spider. "Y-e-l-l-o-w. Yellow."

"Correct," said the principal.

Then the words got a little harder. "February," said the principal. "Soon it will be February." It was Spider's turn again.

"February," said Spider, remembering the *r*. "Capital f-e-b-r-u-a-r-y. February."

"Correct," said the principal.

Finally there were only two spellers left standing—Spider and Elsie, a girl from the other side of the reservation.

"Terrific," said the principal. "We have a terrific basketball team."

"Terrific," said Spider, taking a big breath. "T-e-r-r-i-f-f-i-c. Terrific."

"Incorrect," said the principal. Then she turned to Elsie. "Terrific. We have a terrific basketball team."

"Terrific," said Elsie, "T-e-r-r-i-f-i-c. Terrific."

"Correct," said the principal. "Let's give a hand to our two winners from Miss Phillips' class: Elsie in first place and Spider in second place."

It was over! Spider climbed down the steps and found the rows where his family was sitting. Spider's father shook his hand and Will slapped him on the back. "You did it!" his mother said proudly. "You stood right up there in front of everybody!"

"It was easy," said Spider.

"You were brave," said his father. "Brave as a mountain lion."

"And clever," said his grandmother. "Clever as a coyote."

I wasn't even afraid, Spider thought. I listened to my spirit. "But now I'm hungry," he told his family. "Hungry as a bear. Let's all go home and eat."

About the Author

Ann Herbert Scott

Ann Herbert Scott has been writing for nearly her whole life. Her parents were proud of her special talent and collected her writings in scrapbooks when she was small.

When Ms. Scott was in her teens and twenties, she worked with inner-city children. At the time, there weren't many books about children like those she worked with. This bothered her. "I dreamed that someday I would write true-to-life stories that would be set in the housing project where I worked," she says. Many years later Ms. Scott wrote *Big Cowboy Western* about a boy who lives in the inner city.

Reader Response

Open for Discussion

Spider has stage fright. If you had to get up on stage in front of your whole school, would you be nervous? Why or why not?

Comprehension Check

1. Think of a movie, video, or TV character who is afraid of something. What would Spider say to that character? Use details from the story to support your answer.

2. Look back through the story. Where does Spider change? Do you think Spider will enter any more contests? Why or why not?

3. Look back through the story. List three or four things Spider is advised to be or to do. Which piece of advice would be most helpful to you?

4. Think about the auditorium where the spelling bee takes place. **Visualize** the auditorium and describe it to a friend. What do you see, hear, smell, and feel? (Visualizing)

5. Spider and his family are about to celebrate. **Visualize** the celebration. Give details about what they will eat and what they might talk about. (Visualizing)

Test Prep
Look Back and Write

Look back at pages 345–347. Explain how Spider was brave as a mountain lion, clever as a coyote, and silent as a spider when he entered the spelling bee. Use examples from the story to support your answer.

Technology Connection

Back

Test Prep

How to Read an Internet Article

1. Preview

- You might read an Internet article when you are using a computer. The underlined words are links that lead you to more information. Look at the headings, pictures, and links. Decide what you will read first, next, and last.

2. Read and Use a K-W-L Chart

- Before you read, fill in the **K** and **W** columns of a **K-W-L** chart. As you read, write what you learn in the **L** column.

3. Think and Connect

Think about *Brave as a Mountain Lion*. Then read through your K-W-L chart from "Spiders."

Imagine Spider is your friend. Share with him the most surprising things you learned about spiders. How will this new information change Spider's ideas about Little Spider?

Spiders

by Avocado Elementary School Teachers and Students

This description of a science experiment comes from a World Wide Web site on the Internet.

Experiment

The spiders in the vivariums were used to conduct an experiment. The students were asked to observe the behavior of the spiders in the vivariums for a week. The vivariums where spiders were kept look like aquariums, but without the water.

Question

Do spiders eat only insects?

Hypothesis

We believe that spiders eat only insects.

Avocado Elementary School
Homestead, Florida

Teachers and Staff	Science Inquiry Hotlists
Events	Science Projects
Web Searchers	Technology Projects

Crab Spider

House Spider

Black widow

Observations

The eating habits of the vivarium spiders were observed for a week on a daily basis. The students paid attention to what the spiders would or would not eat. The students charted their observations on a log. Some of the things that were fed to the spiders were dead bugs, ants, and crickets.

The spiders in our observation were:

- Black widows
- Crab spiders
- Banana spiders
- Garden spiders
- House spiders

We found out that spiders not only eat insects, but they also eat other animals. This includes other spiders, birds, and mice.

Conclusion

What we observed disproves our hypothesis.

What We Learned About Spiders

- Spiders are arachnids.
- Their bodies are in two parts, the head and the abdomen.
- They do not have feelers.
- Most spiders have eight eyes, but some have six, four, or two.
- Many spiders trap their food in webs.
- Not all spiders make webs.
- Some spiders dig homes under the ground.
- Some spiders have claws at the ends of their legs.
- Spiders live in all sorts of environments. Some live underwater.

Skill Lesson

Generalizing

- A **generalization** is a statement or rule that applies to many examples.

- You sometimes are given ideas about several things or people. A generalization might say how they are mostly alike or all alike in some way.

- Clue words such as *all, always, everyone, some,* and *never* can signal a generalization.

Read "All About MIMI" from *Mimi's Tutu* by Tynia Thomassie.

Talk About It

1. Look for the clue words *all, always,* and *everyone* in the story. What generalizations does the author make using these words?

2. What generalizations can you make about MIMI's family?

ALL ABOUT MIMI

by Tynia Thomassie

When MIMI was born, she followed a long line of boys. The family rejoiced at the arrival of their first little girl. Especially the grandmothers.

All the grandfathers and uncles had been honored with namesakes. There was Jacques, for Mama's father, and Emile, after Mama's brother. Clarence and Forest were named for Daddy's father and brother. In fact, there were more boys than uncles and grandfathers to name them after.

Now all the grandmothers and aunts felt that the new baby should be named after *them*. But, there were two grandmothers

and two aunts, and only one very small little girl.

That's how she became to be called M'bewe Iecine Magalee Isabella . . . or MIMI for short.

From the time MIMI was a baby, she was always surrounded by music and dance. This was her family's tradition. Grampa Jacques beat out rhythms on the *congas*, while Uncle Forest played the cowbell. Aunt Isabella played the claves and Gramma Iecine shook the brightly beaded *shekere*.

Gramma M'bewe knew the ceremonial dances of Guinea, and Mama was a fine dancer too.

Whenever the family gathered, everyone from the tallest to the smallest grabbed an instrument or danced.

MIMI would bob to the beat or shake her rattle in time to the music.

LOOK AHEAD

Your Dad Was Just Like You
written and illustrated by Dolores Johnson

In *Your Dad Was Just Like You*, a boy, like MIMI, learns that parents and children share many common habits. Read and get ready to make generalizations about the boy, his father, and his grandfather.

Vocabulary

Words to Know

serious	problem	prove
jokes	neighborhood	prize

Words with similar meanings, like *silent* and *quiet,* are called **synonyms.** You can often figure out the meaning of an unknown word by finding a clue in the words around it. This clue may be a synonym.

Read this paragraph. Notice how *show* helps you understand what *prove* means.

More Alike Than Different

My mom and I are very much alike. We both grew up in the same <u>neighborhood</u>, and we both tell <u>jokes</u> when things get too <u>serious</u>. My mother is an award-winning artist, and I won a <u>prize</u> for my painting. We both can solve a math <u>problem</u> easily. Does this show my point? Though sometimes we seem different, these facts <u>prove</u> that we are alike!

Write About It

Describe how you and a family member or friend are alike and different. Use vocabulary words.

Your Dad Was Just Like You

written and illustrated
by Dolores Johnson

Peter stood at the front door of his grandfather's house. "You're the best grandpa that ever was," he said. "Can I move in with you?"

"Move in with me? What happened this time? Did you and your dad have another fight?" asked Peter's grandfather. "You two are always battlin'."

"I wasn't doin' anything, Grandpa," said Peter. "I was just playing around—you know—running, and that ole stupid purple thing on Dad's dresser just seemed to jump onto the floor and break. Dad was so mad, he didn't even yell. He was so mad, he just walked away. Grandpa, I think I need to move in with you."

"Dad was so mad, he didn't even yell."

"Why don't we take a walk, Grandson, and sort this problem out? Sometimes my head works better when my legs get a chance to stretch."

The two walked through the neighborhood their family had lived in for years. After they had walked some, Peter sighed, "I wish Dad was more like you, Grandpa. He never smiles—he only yells. 'Look at these awful grades, Peter.' 'You never finish anything you start, Peter.' 'Why can't you be more serious, Peter?' He just never leaves me alone."

"There was a time when your father laughed and smiled all the time," said Peter's grandfather. "When he was a boy, your dad was just like you."

"My daddy was a *boy* . . . just like *me?*" asked Peter.

"That boy would tell me silly jokes just like you tell. When I didn't even feel like smiling, that boy sure could make me laugh. All he had to do was tell his favorite knock knock jokes."

"*My* dad told *knock knock* jokes?" asked Peter. "You sure you're talking about *my* dad?"

"I know it's hard for you to believe," said his grandfather, "but when your father was young, he was like any other boy. Sometimes he played so long at this park, I almost had to drag him home. He played basketball on that court until he almost wore out the net. He even led big game safaris through that jungle gym."

"Dad played in *my* jungle?" asked Peter.

"He played combat with little green army men on the grass by those swings. He practically wore a groove in this sidewalk with his bicycle. But there was one thing that boy loved to do more than anything else in the world."

"My daddy was a boy... just like me?"

"What's that, Grandpa?" Peter chuckled. "Yell at the little kids? Start fights?"

"More than living, laughing, or eating, your father loved to run. He ran from sunup to sundown. He ran so fast that his shadow had trouble keeping up with him."

Peter asked, "So why doesn't my dad run now?"

"There came a time when he became serious. And he told himself, a serious man doesn't run."

"Did he ever run in a race?" asked Peter. "Did he ever win a prize?"

"Your father ran only one race, when he wasn't much older than you. It was the biggest race in the town for schoolkids. Your father sure wanted to win that big golden trophy."

"Dad must have lost the race, 'cause I've never seen any big golden trophy. At least not on the bookshelf where he keeps all his special stuff."

"Sometimes you don't compete for trophies just to place them high up on a shelf," said his grandfather. "Sometimes you compete so you can prove something to yourself. When your father was your age, he had something to prove. He was having trouble in school. Nothing seemed to be going right for him."

"Did he win, Grandpa?"

"But my daddy's so smart!" said Peter.

"He didn't think he was smart, but he *knew* he was fast. He could run like the wind, and he wanted to show everyone. He stopped playing games. He stopped laughing and joking. He ran day and night as fast as he could because he wanted to run that race and win."

"Did he win, Grandpa?"

Peter's grandfather laughed. "Are you going to let me tell my story? Everyone from town—hundreds of people—lined every inch of that one-mile course to the courthouse. About fifty boys and girls gathered at the starting line, fidgeting and milling about like pigeons on a telephone wire. The starter raised his gun. 'On your mark . . . get set . . .' he thundered. And then the worst thing that could possibly happen happened."

"What, Grandpa?"

"A drop of rain fell, and then another and another."

"It started raining?" laughed Peter. "So? I've run a million times in the rain."

"Not rain like this, boy. I looked up, and the sky had turned dark and angry. Rain poured down, and pools of water formed at my feet. The starter didn't have to say 'Go!' because the children had already started running. But they weren't running to the finish line. They were trying to find the last dry spot on earth."

"So Daddy ran for cover too, huh, Grandpa? You know, he doesn't like to mess up his clothes."

"No. It seems your father had something he just had to do. He picked up one leg after the other and ran as fast as he could toward the end of the race.

"And he kept running even though the rain came down so heavy it nearly knocked him down with its force. The wind howled around him, and pools of water were reaching up to drag at his feet."

"Did Daddy ever reach the finish line?"

"Yes, Grandson, but no one was there to congratulate him. No one handed him a big trophy. No one told him how good he was."

"Where were you, Grandpa?"

"I ran behind your father. I didn't catch up to him until the very end. I finally reached him as he stood alone, shaking his head and sobbing in the rain."

"So what did you do, Grandpa?"

"I picked your father up and carried him home. I dried him off and laid him down. And while he probably cried himself to sleep, I sat down with these two big, clumsy hands of mine and made my boy a trophy, because he really deserved one."

"So where is the trophy now, Grandpa?"

"Well, it . . . it was . . ." said the old man.

"Was it a big ole stupid purple . . . ? Oh, I'm sorry, Grandpa. What did Dad say when you gave it to him?"

"He didn't really say much at all . . . just, 'I love you, Dad,' for the very first time. You see, when

your father was a boy, he and I used to fight a lot. I used to yell at him. I hardly ever smiled. We decided to change what was wrong between us. That day, we became a real serious father and son."

"I've got to go home now, Grandpa. There's something serious I've got to do," said Peter. He hugged his grandfather tightly, and then ran the short distance home.

When Peter got home, he gathered the purple pieces that still lay in a heap in his father's bedroom. Then the boy brought them to his own bedroom and worked very hard to make what was broken whole again.

Peter stood in the doorway of the living room and watched his father read in silence. Then the little boy said just three words, even though he was so nervous he felt like running away. "Knock, knock, Dad."

His father hesitated for just a moment, looked up, smiled, and said, "Who's there?"

Then the boy . . . **worked very hard** to make what was broken **whole** again.

About the Author/Illustrator
Dolores Johnson

Dolores Johnson was an artist and didn't know it. "When I was young," she says, "I knew I could draw, but I didn't think I was an artist." She knew her

brother was an artist, because he was always drawing or painting. But she liked things besides art too.

So when they grew up, Ms. Johnson's brother got a job as an artist. She herself tried many different jobs but kept working on art projects at night. One day a friend saw some of her paintings and writings. She told Ms. Johnson that she should create a children's book. Five years later, her illustrations were published in her first book. Now she writes the words for many of her books too.

Ms. Johnson remembers how things felt when she was a child and writes about those feelings. She writes about how it feels to go to a baby-sitter, to come home to an empty house, or to have trouble getting along with someone you love.

Now Ms. Johnson knows that she is an artist, and she loves being one. She feels a great responsibility to the children who read her books. "I hope that they might find as much pleasure reading my books as I have writing them," she says.

...I didn't think I was an artist.

Reader Response

Open for Discussion
What happens when someone breaks something that belongs to someone else? How do the people feel? What should each one do?

Comprehension Check

1. Look back through the story. In what ways are Peter and his dad alike?

2. Spider in *Brave as a Mountain Lion* comes in second in the spelling bee, and Dad as a boy doesn't even get to race. Compare how the two boys must have felt. Support your answer with details from the stories.

3. Look back at page 369. What do you think will happen after Peter gives the mended trophy to Dad?

4. Think about both Spider and Dad. Make a **generalization** about how important a contest can be. (Generalizing)

5. Think about what the story tells about how Peter and Dad get along, and also about how Dad and Grandpa got along. What can you **generalize** about how some fathers and sons get along? (Generalizing)

Test Prep
Look Back and Write
Look back at the beginning of the story. Use details to explain why Peter wants to live with his grandfather.

Games and Sports

by A. Langley & M. Butterfield

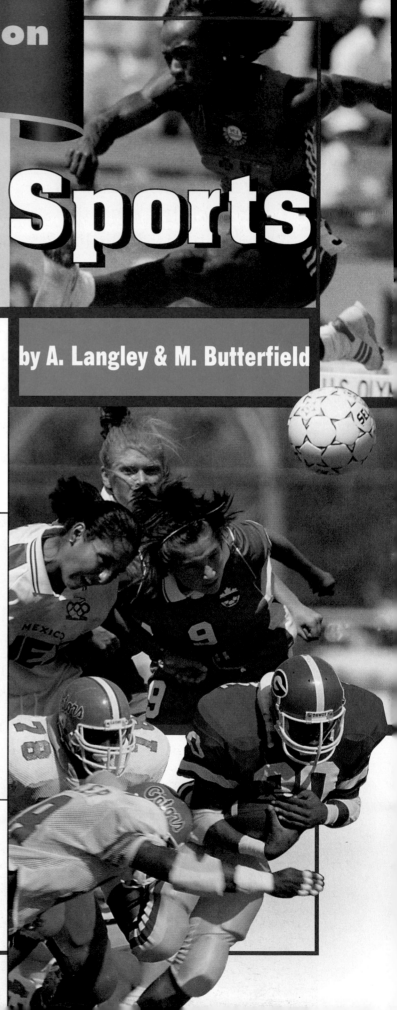

There are hundreds of different sports and games. People play some of them all over the world, while others are traditional local games that have never spread beyond the country where they were first invented.

Soccer may be the most popular sport in the world. Its present form began in England in the 19th century. Today, almost every country has a national team.

Several games grew out of soccer. In rugby football and American football, players run with an oval ball. In Australian football, the ball can be punched, bounced, or kicked.

The Iroquois Indians of North America play a winter sport called snow-snakes. The spear "snakes" can speed up to 120 mph (193 kph) and travel well over a mile.

The fastest sport in the world is probably jai alai, a kind of tennis played in the Basque region of Europe and in Latin America.

Jai alai players have a large scoop-shaped racket on one hand. The idea is to hit a rubber ball against three walls.

National Games

The traditional sport of Japan is sumo wrestling. The wrestlers must train hard for many years and they must also eat hard! The aim of the fight is to force your opponent to the ground or out of the ring. So sumo wrestlers are very heavy and hard to move. Most of them weigh over 280 pounds (127 kg).

People in Argentina, India, Great Britain, and other countries play polo, a type of hockey on horseback. The players use long sticks with mallet heads to hit a wooden ball around the field. Polo fields can measure up to 300 yards (270 m) long and 200 yards (180 m) wide.

The national game of Canada is ice hockey. The country's frozen lakes and harbors were the first playing rinks.

Each team has six players who are well padded for protection. The idea is to try to flick a puck into the goal with their sticks.

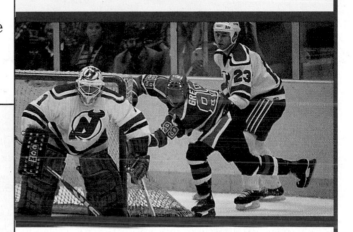

Olympic Games

Athletes from every nation take part in the Olympic Games, held every four years. The modern games began in 1896, modeled after the ancient Greek games at Olympia, Greece.

At the Olympic opening ceremony, all the participants parade in the stadium. A torchbearer lights the Olympic flame that burns throughout the games. A relay of runners brings the torch all the way from Olympia.

373

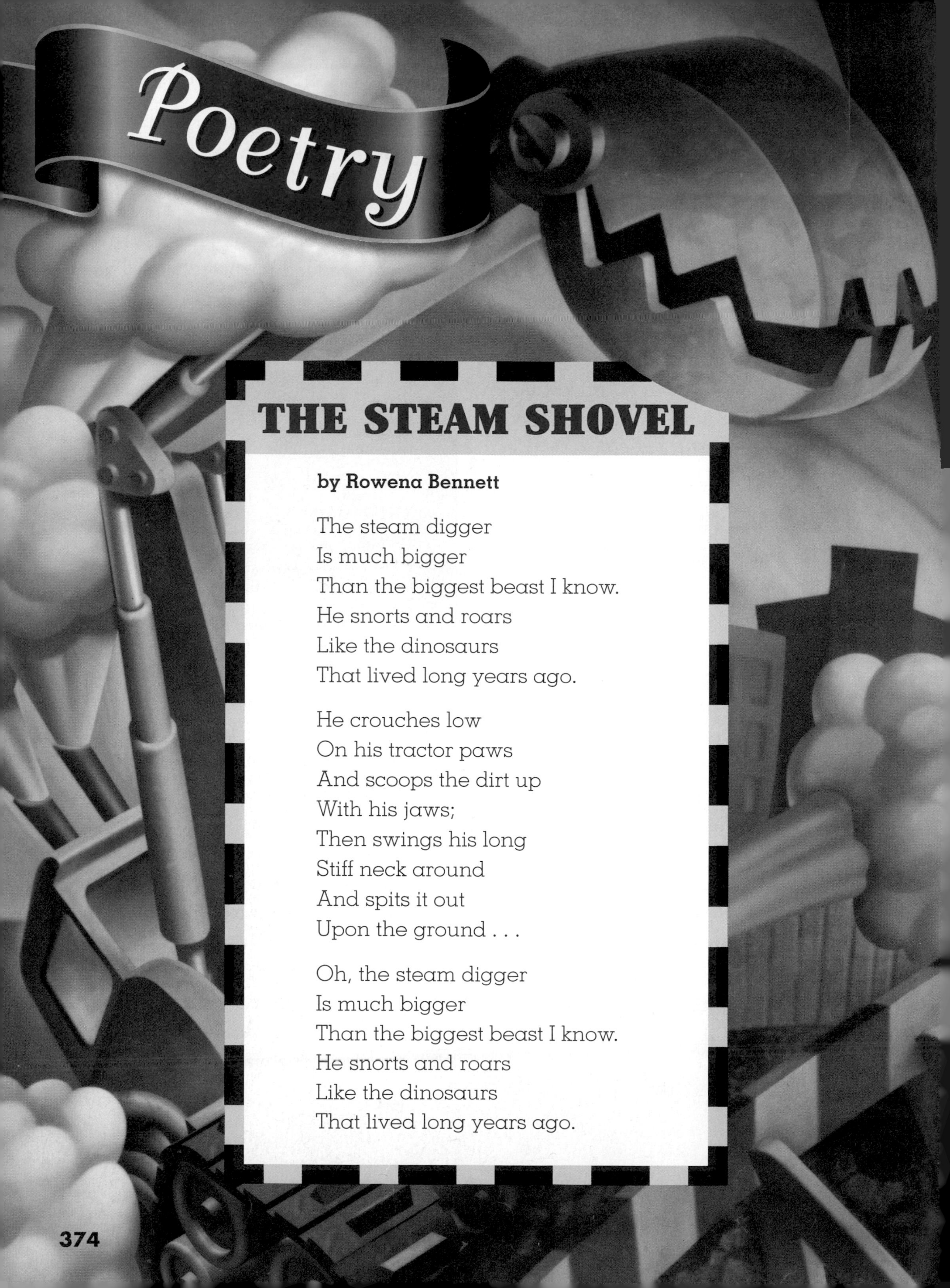

THE STEAM SHOVEL

by Rowena Bennett

The steam digger
Is much bigger
Than the biggest beast I know.
He snorts and roars
Like the dinosaurs
That lived long years ago.

He crouches low
On his tractor paws
And scoops the dirt up
With his jaws;
Then swings his long
Stiff neck around
And spits it out
Upon the ground . . .

Oh, the steam digger
Is much bigger
Than the biggest beast I know.
He snorts and roars
Like the dinosaurs
That lived long years ago.

VACUUM CLEANER

by Sylvia Cassedy

Like some greased beast
released
all at once
from its cave,
here comes the vacuum
   cleaner!

Slipping the lip
of its leathery trunk
high, low,
over, below,
it eats its lunch:

Munches on chunks of
jangling junk;
gulps down hunks of
   purple pulp;

Feeds on clumps of
seeds, of beads;
pecks at specks of
lint, of wool;

Picks at thick gray
wads of stuff:
dust,
hair,
spider fluff.

Crops, sips,
sucks, laps,
until, at last,
its belly full,
it backs itself
into its lair.

Lineage

by Margaret Walker

My grandmothers were strong.
They followed plows and bent to toil.
They moved through fields sowing seed.
They touched earth and grain grew.
They were full of sturdiness and singing.
My grandmothers were strong.

My grandmothers are full of memories.
Smelling of soap and onions and wet clay
With veins rolling roughly over quick hands
They have many clean words to say.
My grandmothers were strong.
Why am I not as they?

HONOR

by Alma Flor Ada

Honor is the work
we do in the fields.
Honor is a family
who loves and cares for one another.
Honor is being true to myself
as I wake up each morning.

HONOR

por Alma Flor Ada

Honor es el trabajo
que hacemos en los campos.
Honor es la familia
que se quiere y se apoya.
Honor es ser quien soy,
al despertar cada mañana.

Wrap-Up

How can we learn from everything we do?

RIDE A BIKE

FIRST STEPS

START

1ST GRADE

GO BACK

SEE FIRST BIG LEAGUE GAME

A Bestseller

Make a Book Cover

Which selection in Unit 3 taught you something important?

1. **Choose** a selection that taught you a new idea or a lesson. Reread it.

2. **Fold** a sheet of paper in half to make a book cover. Choose a character, object, or scene to draw on the front. Include the title and author's name.

3. **Write** what you learned and why it is important on the back. Include a quotation from the selection.

3RD GRADE

Like Father, Like Son

Act Out What Happens Next

In the last picture of *Your Dad Was Just Like You*, Peter stands in front of his dad with the mended trophy behind his back. What do you think Peter and his dad will do next?

1. **Reread** the story with a partner.

2. **Choose** who will play each part.

3. **Act out** what you think will happen next.

And the Winner Is . . .

Create a Medal for a Winner

Spider is brave in *Brave as a Mountain Lion*. Ursula is a good dog guide in *Mom's Best Friend*.

1. **Compare** the accomplishments of Spider and Ursula. Then choose one to honor with a medal.

2. **Design** your medal. Think of a shape and color to represent your winner.

3. **Create** the medal and add words of praise.

Once Upon a Time

Choose a Character and Retell

What would Bear tell his grandchildren about his friend Hare in *Tops and Bottoms?* What would Hare tell his grandchildren?

1. **Choose** a character. Decide how the character would talk.

2. **Reread** the story as if you are the character.

3. **Retell** the story to a small group. Imagine they are your grandchildren.

Test Talk

Answer the Question

Make the Right Choice

Before you can answer a multiple-choice test question, you have to decide on the best answer. A test about "Super Senses," pages 281–283, might have this question.

Test Question 1

What is alike about how bats and whales hear?

Ⓐ They listen for rustling noises.

Ⓑ Whales hear under water.

Ⓒ They listen to sounds bounce off objects.

Ⓓ Bats hang upside-down.

Understand the question. Find the key words. Finish the statement "I need to find out . . ."

Narrow the answer choices. Read each answer choice carefully. Rule out any choice that you know is wrong.

Look back at the text. Is the answer *right there* in one place in the text or do you have to *think and search?* Does the answer depend on the *author and you?*

Choose the best answer. Mark the answer. Check it by comparing it with the text.

See how one student makes the right choice.

Answer **B** only talks about whales, and answer **D** only talks about bats. So the answer must be **A** or **C**. I'm not sure, so I'll go back and look at the article.

Since I need to find out how bats and whales hear, I'll go back to the part called "Hearing." I see the words **bats** and **whales**. The sentence says, "Bats and whales find their way around by listening to sounds bounce off objects." That's the same as answer **C**. The right answer must be **C**.

Try it!

Now decide on the best answer to these test questions about "Super Senses," pages 281–283.

Test Question 2

Look at the picture of the dog on page 283. Why is the arrow pointing to the dog's nose?

(A) to show what the dog's nose looks like

(B) to show where the dog's nose is

(C) to show that the dog uses its mouth to taste

(D) to show that the dog uses its nose to smell

Test Question 3

What is the main idea of "Super Senses"?

(F) Animals have five senses.

(G) Animals have similar senses, but most have developed certain senses to meet their needs.

(H) Moles don't need to have good eyesight.

(I) People have five senses.

Glossary

How to Use This Glossary

This glossary can help you understand and pronounce some of the words in this book. The entries in this glossary are in alphabetical order. There are guide words at the top of each page to show you the first and last words on the page. A pronunciation key is at the bottom of every other page. Remember, if you can't find the word you are looking for, ask for help or check a dictionary.

The entry word is in dark type. It shows how the word is spelled and how the word is divided into syllables.

The pronunciation is in parentheses. It also shows which syllables are stressed.

Part-of-speech labels show the function or functions of an entry word and any listed form of that word.

ap•ply (ə plī′), VERB. to put on: *Apply another coat of paint after the first one has dried.* ❏ VERB **ap•plies, ap•plied, ap•ply•ing.**

Sometimes, irregular and other forms will be shown to help you use the word correctly.

The definition and example sentence show you what the word means and how it is used.

Aa

a•fraid (ə frād′), ADJECTIVE. frightened; feeling fear: *She was afraid of fire.*

aim (ām), VERB. to point or direct something at a goal or target: *She aimed the arrow at the target.* ❏ VERB **aims, aimed, aim•ing.**

a•larm (ə lärm′), VERB. to make afraid; frighten: *The sudden noise alarmed me.* ❏ VERB **a•larms, a•larmed, a•larm•ing.**

a•lert (ə lėrt′), ADJECTIVE. watchful; wide-awake: *The dog was alert to every sound.*

an•chor (ang′kər), VERB. to set in place; attach firmly: *The campers anchor their tent to the ground.* ❏ VERB **an•chors, an•chored, an•chor•ing.**

ap•ply (ə plī′), VERB. to put on: *Apply another coat of paint after the first one has dried.* ❏ VERB **ap•plies, ap•plied, ap•ply•ing.**

au•thor (o'thər), NOUN. someone who writes books, poems, stories, or articles; writer: *She is one of my favorite authors.*

author

B b

bac•ter•i•a (bak tir'ē ə), NOUN. very tiny and simple living things, so small that they can usually only be seen through a microscope. Some bacteria cause diseases such as pneumonia; others do useful things, such as turning cider into vinegar. ❑ SINGULAR **bac•ter•i•um** (bak tir' ē əm).

bas•ket•ball (bas'kit bȯl'), NOUN.
1 a game played with a large, round ball between two teams of five players each. The players score points by tossing the ball through baskets hanging at either end of the court.
2 the ball used in this game.

bounce (bouns), VERB.
1 to spring into the air like a ball: *The baby likes to bounce up and down on the bed.*
2 to cause to bounce: *She bounced the ball to me.*
❑ VERB **bounc•es, bounced, bounc•ing.**

bound¹ (bound), VERB. to leap or spring lightly along; jump: *The mountain goat bounded from rock to rock.* ❑ VERB **bounds, bound•ed, bound•ing.**

bound² (bound), VERB. to form the boundary of; limit: *The United States is bounded by Canada on the north.* ❑ VERB **bounds, bound•ed, bound•ing.**

brave (brāv), ADJECTIVE. without fear; showing courage: *The brave woman went into the burning house to save a baby.* ❑ ADJECTIVE **brav•er, brav•est.**

a hat	ė term	ô order	ch child	(a in about
ā age	i it	oi oil	ng long	e in taken
ä far	ī ice	ou out	sh she	ə { i in pencil
â care	o hot	u cup	th thin	o in lemon
e let	ō open	u̇ put	ᴛʜ then	(u in circus
ē equal	ȯ saw	ü rule	zh measure	

383

break (brāk),

1 *VERB.* to come apart or make come apart: *This cheap toy breaks easily.*
2 *NOUN.* a broken place; crack: *There was a break in the wall. The X ray showed a break in my leg.* ❏ *VERB* **breaks, broke, bro·ken, break·ing.**

break·fast (brek′fəst), *NOUN.* the first meal of the day.

breathe (brēᴛʜ), *VERB.* to draw air into the lungs and force it out. You breathe through your nose or through your mouth. ❏ *VERB* **breathes, breathed, breath·ing.**

bur·ro (bėr′ō), *NOUN.* a donkey used to carry loads or packs in the southwestern United States and Mexico. ❏ *PLURAL* **bur·ros.** ■ Another word that sounds like this is **burrow.**

bur·row (bėr′ō), *NOUN.* a hole dug in the ground by an animal for shelter or protection. Rabbits live in burrows. ■ Another word that sounds like this is **burro.**

busi·ness (biz′nis), *NOUN.* work done to earn a living; occupation: *A carpenter's business is building things.* ❏ *PLURAL* **busi·ness·es.**

Cc

card·board (kärd′bôrd′), *NOUN.* a stiff material made of layers of paper pulp pressed together, used to make cards, boxes, and so on.

cheat (chēt), *VERB.* to deceive or trick someone; do business or play in a way that is not honest: *I refused to play the game with her because she cheated.* ❏ *VERB* **cheats, cheat·ed, cheat·ing. –cheat·er,** *NOUN.*

chic·or·y (chik′ər ē), *NOUN.* a plant with bright blue flowers and leaves that are used for salad: *The cooks often used chicory and lettuce in their salads.*

clev·er (klev′ər), *ADJECTIVE.* bright; intelligent; having a quick mind: *She is the cleverest person in our class.*

cliff (klif), *NOUN.* a very steep, rocky slope.

col·lect (kə lekt′), *VERB.* to bring things together; gather together: *Our teacher will collect our homework this morning.* ❏ *VERB* **col·lects, col·lect·ed, col·lect·ing.**

com·fort·a·ble (kum′fər tə bəl), *ADJECTIVE.* giving comfort: *A soft, warm bed is comfortable.*

comfortable

con·cen·trate (kon′sən trat), *VERB.* to pay close attention: *I will concentrate on my reading so that I understand the story.* ❏ *VERB* **con·cen·trates, con·cen·trat·ed, con·cen·trat·ing.**

con·fi·dent (kon′fə dənt), *ADJECTIVE.* firmly believing; certain; sure: *I feel confident that our team will win.*

cor·rect (kə rekt′), *VERB.* to change something to a better condition or to agree with some standard: *Your manners need some correcting.* ❏ *VERB* **cor·rects, cor·rect·ed, cor·rect·ing.**

cough (kȯf), *VERB.* to force air out of your throat with a loud noise: *He coughs when there is dust in the air.* ❏ *VERB* **coughs, coughed, cough·ing.**

cow·boy (kou′boi′), *NOUN.* a man who works on a cattle ranch or at rodeos: *Several cowboys worked on our ranch.*

co·zy (kō′zē), *ADJECTIVE.* warm and comfortable; snug: *The cat lay in a cozy corner near the fireplace.* ❏ *ADJECTIVE* **co·zi·er, co·zi·est.**

cre·vasse (krə vas′), *NOUN.* a deep crack or split in the ice of a glacier: *The climbers did not want to fall into the crevasse.*

cur·i·ous (kyùr′ē əs), *ADJECTIVE.* eager to know: *Small children are very curious, and they ask many questions.*

a	hat	ė	term	ô	order	ch	child	ə	a in about
ā	age	i	it	oi	oil	ng	long		e in taken
ä	far	ī	ice	ou	out	sh	she		i in pencil
â	care	o	hot	u	cup	th	thin		o in lemon
e	let	ō	open	ù	put	ŦH	then		u in circus
ē	equal	ȯ	saw	ü	rule	zh	measure		

D d

de·bunk (dē bungk′), VERB. to uncover, or make known, false information: *The article debunked the belief that you should try to outrun a tornado.* ❏ VERB **de·bunks, de·bunked, de·bunk·ing.**

de·stroy (di stroi′), VERB. to damage something very badly; ruin or smash: *A tornado can destroy a house.* ❏ VERB **de·stroys, de·stroyed, de·stroy·ing.**

destroy

dif·fi·cult (dif′ə kult), ADJECTIVE.
1 hard to do or understand: *Math is difficult for some students.*
2 hard to deal with or get along with; not easy to please: *My cousin is difficult and is always unhappy.*

di·lute (də lüt′), VERB. to make something weaker or thinner by adding water or some other liquid: *I diluted the frozen orange juice with two cans of water.* ❏ VERB **di·lutes, di·lut·ed, di·lut·ing.**

di·rec·tion (də rek′shən), NOUN. any way in which you may face, point, or go: *Please point me in the direction of the cafeteria.*

dis·cov·er (dis kuv′ər), VERB. to find out something that was not known before: *Scientists have discovered a new type of medicine.* ❏ VERB **dis·cov·ers, dis·cov·ered, dis·cov·er·ing.**

dream (drēm), NOUN.
1 thoughts, feelings, and mental images during sleep: *I had a bad dream last night.*
2 something like a dream; daydream; wish: *I have dreams of becoming a famous scientist.*

E e

eas·i·ly (ē′zə lē), ADVERB. without trying hard; with little effort: *The simple tasks were easily done.*

ed·i·ble (ed′ə bəl), ADJECTIVE. safe or good to eat: *Toadstools are not edible.*

e·gret (ē′gret), NOUN. a wading bird with a long neck and a long bill. Egrets are usually white. They are a type of heron.

em·bod·y (em bod′ ē), VERB. to put an idea into a form that can be seen: *The building embodied the idea of its architect.* ❏ VERB **em·bod·ies, em·bod·ied, em·bod·y·ing.**

en·vi·ron·ment (en vī′rən mənt), NOUN. all the surrounding things, conditions, and influences affecting the growth of living things, especially air, water, and soil: *Both fish and turtles live in underwater environments.*

e·quip (i kwip′), VERB. to supply someone or something with something that is needed or wanted; supply with all that is needed: *The scouts equipped themselves with canteens and food for the hike.* ❏ VERB **e·quips, e·quipped, e·quip·ping.**

ex·per·i·ment (ek sper′ə mənt), NOUN. a carefully planned trial or test to find out something: *We made an experiment to learn the weight of the air in a basketball.*

eye (ī), NOUN.
1 the part of the body that people and animals use for seeing.
2 the calm, clear area at the center of a hurricane.

a	hat	ė	term	ô	order	ch	child	ə	a in about
ā	age	i	it	oi	oil	ng	long		e in taken
ä	far	ī	ice	ou	out	sh	she		i in pencil
â	care	o	hot	u	cup	th	thin		o in lemon
e	let	ō	open	ù	put	ᴛʜ	then		u in circus
ē	equal	ò	saw	ü	rule	zh	measure		

F f

fa•vor•ite (fā′vər it), ADJECTIVE. liked better than others: *What is your favorite flower? My favorite sports are soccer and softball.*

fo•rest (fôr′ist), NOUN. a large area with many tall trees; thick woods: *Many animals live in the forest.*

G g

gen•ius (jē′nyəs), NOUN. very great mental skill and ability: *Important discoveries are often made by people of genius.*

germ (jėrm), NOUN. a very tiny, simple living thing that often causes disease. Viruses and bacteria are germs.

gift (gift), NOUN. something given; present: *I saved my allowance to buy my sister a birthday gift.*

gob•ble¹ (gob′əl), VERB. to eat very quickly: *The children gobbled their candy.* ❏ VERB **gob•bles, gob•bled, gob•bling.**

gob•ble² (gob′əl),
1 NOUN. the noise a turkey makes.
2 VERB. to make this noise or one like it. ❏ VERB **gob•bles, gob•bled, gob•bling.**

grand•fa•ther (grand′fä′ᴛʜər), NOUN. the father of your father or mother.

guide (gīd), NOUN. someone or something that shows the way: *The guide led us on a trail through the woods.* ❏ PLURAL **guides.**

H h

har•ness (här′nis), NOUN. the leather straps, bands, and other pieces used to hitch a horse or other animal to a carriage, wagon, or plow. ❏ PLURAL **har•ness•es.**

har•vest (här′vist), VERB. to gather crops: *We are harvesting the corn this month.* ❏ VERB **har•vests, har•vest•ed, har•vest•ing.**

hatch (hach), VERB. to come out of an egg: *The chicks should hatch today.* ❏ VERB **hatch·es, hatched, hatch·ing.**

hatch

her·on (her′ ən), NOUN. a wading bird with a long neck, a long bill, and long legs: *They watched the herons wade into the shallow water.*

hinge (hinj), NOUN. a joint on which a door, gate, cover, or lid moves back and forth so that it can open and close.

hun·gry (hung′grē), ADJECTIVE. feeling a need to eat: *I missed breakfast and was hungry all morning.* ❏ ADJECTIVE **hun·gri·er, hun·gri·est.**

hur·ri·cane (her′ə kān), NOUN. a fierce storm with very strong, dangerous winds and, usually, very heavy rain. The wind in a hurricane blows at more than 75 miles per hour.

hy·poth·e·sis (hī poth′ə sis), NOUN. something assumed to be true because it seems likely; theory: *Before the experiment, we formed a hypothesis of what we expected to observe.* ❏ PLURAL **hy·poth·e·ses** (hī poth′ə sēz′).

I i

i·mag·i·na·tion (i maj′ə nā′shən), NOUN. the power to make pictures or ideas in the mind of things not present to the senses. A poet, artist, or inventor must have imagination to create new things or ideas or to combine old ones in new forms.

in·for·ma·tion (in′fər mā′shən), NOUN. knowledge given or received of some fact or event; news: *An encyclopedia contains much information.*

a hat	ė term	ô order	ch child	a in about
ā age	i it	oi oil	ng long	e in taken
ä far	ī ice	ou out	sh she	ə ⟨ i in pencil
â care	o hot	u cup	th thin	o in lemon
e let	ō open	ủ put	ᴛʜ then	u in circus
ē equal	ȯ saw	ü rule	zh measure	

in•sect (in′sekt), NOUN. any of a group of very small animals without bones, with bodies divided into three parts. Insects have three pairs of legs and one or two pairs of wings. Flies, mosquitoes, butterflies, beetles, and bees are insects.

insects

in•tro•duce (in′trə düs′), VERB. to tell people each other's names when they don't know each other: *I will introduce my new friend to my family.* ❏ VERB **in•tro•duc•es, in•tro•duced, in•tro•duc•ing.**

is•land (ī′lənd), NOUN. a body of land surrounded by water: *Hawaii is made up of a group of islands.*

J j

jai a•lai (hī′ä lī′), NOUN. game played on a walled court with a hard ball. In jai alai, the ball is caught and thrown with a kind of curved basket attached to the arm.

joke (jōk), NOUN. a short, funny story you tell to make people laugh: *He told several jokes at the party.*

L l

la•zy (lā′zē), ADJECTIVE. not willing to work or move fast: *He lost his job because he was lazy.* ❏ ADJECTIVE **la•zi•er, la•zi•est.**

li•brar•y (lī′brer′ē), NOUN. a room or building where a collection of books, magazines, films, or recordings is kept for public use and borrowing: *We checked three libraries before we found the book.* ❏ PLURAL **li•brar•ies.**

Mm

marsh (märsh), NOUN. low, soft land covered at times by water, where grasses and reeds but not trees grow: *They explored the wet marshes.* ❑ PLURAL **marsh·es. –marsh·like,** ADJECTIVE.

meas·ured (mezh′ərd), ADJECTIVE. regular; always the same: *She could hear the slow, measured sound of the music.*

melt (melt), VERB. to turn something from a solid into a liquid by heating it. Ice becomes water when it melts. ❑ VERB **melts, melt·ed, melt·ing.**

mu·se·um (myü zē′əm), NOUN. a building for displaying a collection of objects illustrating science, ancient life, art, or other subjects: *We visited two museums to see their new displays.*

Nn

neigh·bor·hood (nā′bər hùd), NOUN. people living near one another: *The whole neighborhood came to the big party.*

noise (noiz), NOUN. an unpleasant or disturbing sound: *The noise kept me awake all night.*

Oo

ob·ser·va·tion (ob′zər vā′shən), NOUN. something seen and noted: *During science experiments, she kept careful records of her observations.*

o·cean (ō′shən), NOUN. the great body of salt water that covers almost three fourths of the Earth's surface; the sea.

op·po·nent (ə pō′ nənt), NOUN. someone who is on the other side in a fight, contest, or discussion: *She beat her opponent in the election.*

a	hat	ė	term	ô	order	ch	child		a in about
ā	age	i	it	oi	oil	ng	long		e in taken
ä	far	ī	ice	ou	out	sh	she	ə	i in pencil
â	care	o	hot	u	cup	th	thin		o in lemon
e	let	ō	open	ù	put	ᵺ	then		u in circus
ē	equal	ò	saw	ü	rule	zh	measure		

391

P p

pale (pāl), *ADJECTIVE.* without much color. *When you have been ill, your face can be pale.*

par•a•site (par′ ə sīt), *NOUN.* a living thing that spends its life on or in another living thing, from which it gets its food, often harming the other living thing. A flea is a parasite that can live on a dog.

part•ner (pärt′nər), *NOUN.* a member of a company who shares the risks and profits of the business: *Three business partners bought my mother's old company.*

paste (pāst), *VERB.* to stick things together with glue: *Paste the orange paper onto the black paper.* ❏ *VERB* **pastes, past•ed, past•ing.**

pa•tient (pā′shənt), *ADJECTIVE.* able to wait quietly for something that you want: *We need to be patient while we are standing in line.*

pitch•er (pich′ər), *NOUN.* a container with a lip at one side and a handle at the other. Pitchers are used for holding and pouring out liquids.

plan•et (plan′it), *NOUN.* one of the nine large astronomical objects that move around the sun. Mercury, Venus, Earth, Mars, Jupiter, Saturn, Uranus, Neptune, and Pluto are planets.

planet

plant (plant), *NOUN.* any living thing that can make its own food from sunlight, air, and water. Plants cannot move about by themselves. Trees, bushes, vines, grass, vegetables, and seaweed are all plants.

play•ground (plā′ground′), *NOUN.* a place to play outdoors.

po•em (pō′əm), NOUN. a piece of writing that expresses the writer's imagination. In poems, the patterns made by the sounds of the words have special importance.

po•li•o (pō′ lē ō), NOUN. a disease that causes fever, loss of the ability to move various muscles, and sometimes death. Polio is now very rare.

pol•len (pol′ ən), NOUN. a fine yellow powder carried by bees from flower to flower. Pollen fertilizes the female cells, or parts, of plants.

pow•er•ful (pou′ər fəl), ADJECTIVE. having great power or force; strong: *The principal is a powerful person. My illness improved after the doctor gave me some powerful medicine.*

prac•tice (prak′tis), NOUN. an action done many times over to gain skill: *Practice makes perfect.*

pre•pare (pri pâr′), VERB. to get something ready; to get yourself ready for doing something: *We all helped prepare a picnic lunch. When the bell rings, we all prepare to go outside.* ❑ VERB **pre•pares, pre•pared, pre•par•ing.**

pre•tend (pri tend′), VERB. to make believe something, just for fun: *Let's pretend that we are grown-ups.* ❑ VERB **pre•tends, pre•tend•ed, pre•tend•ing.**

prim•i•tive (prim′ ə tiv), ADJECTIVE. of or about times long ago: *Primitive people often lived in caves.* **prim•i•tive•ness,** NOUN.

prize (priz), NOUN. something you win for doing something well; reward: *Prizes will be given for the best stories.*

prob•lem (prob′ləm), NOUN. a question or situation, especially a difficult one: *Poverty is a national problem.*

a	hat	ė	term	ô	order	ch	child	ə	a in about
ā	age	i	it	oi	oil	ng	long		e in taken
ä	far	ī	ice	ou	out	sh	she		i in pencil
â	care	o	hot	u	cup	th	thin		o in lemon
e	let	ō	open	ù	put	ŦH	then		u in circus
ē	equal	ò	saw	ü	rule	zh	measure		

393

prom·ise (prom′is), VERB. to say or write that you will do or will not do something: *I promise to come to your party.* ❑ VERB **prom·is·es, prom·ised, prom·is·ing.**

prove (prüv), VERB. to show that something is true: *Prove your statement.* ❑ VERB **proves, proved, proved** or **prov·en, prov·ing.**

R r

re·cep·tor (ri sep′ tər), NOUN. a nerve cell or group of nerve cells sensitive to light, heat, taste, touch, or movement: *Her taste receptors told her that the candy was sweet.*

re·li·a·ble (ri lī′ ə bəl), ADJECTIVE. able to be depended on: *Send her to the bank for the money; she is reliable and honest.* **–re·li′a·bil′·i·ty,** NOUN. **re·li′·a·bly,** ADVERB.

res·er·va·tion (rez′ər vā′shən), NOUN. land set aside by the government for a special purpose: *My aunt is a doctor on an Indian reservation.*

ro·de·o (rō′dē ō *or* rō dā′ō), NOUN. a contest or show in which cowboys and cowgirls show their skills. They ride wild horses, steers, and bulls, and rope cattle. ❑ PLURAL **ro·de·os.**

rus·tling (rus′ ling), NOUN. a light, soft sound of things gently rubbing together: *The breeze caused a rustling of leaves.* ❑ VERB **rus·tles, rus·tled, rus·tling.**

S s

scar·y (skâr′ē), ADJECTIVE. making someone feel afraid: *We watched a scary movie.* ❑ ADJECTIVE **scar·i·er, scar·i·est. –scar′i·ness,** NOUN.

search (sėrch), VERB. to look through; go over carefully; examine, especially for something hidden: *The police are searching the prisoners to see if they have weapons.* ❑ VERB **search·es, searched, search·ing.**

se·cret (sē′krit), ADJECTIVE. kept from the knowledge of others: *The army had a secret plan to win the war.*

ser·i·ous (sir′ē əs), ADJECTIVE. thoughtful; not humorous: *We had a serious discussion about classroom safety.*

sheet (shēt), NOUN.
1 a large piece of cloth, usually of linen or cotton, used on a bed to sleep on or under.
2 a single piece of paper.

shoot (shüt), VERB. to send a ball, puck, or the like toward the goal while scoring or trying to score: *We went to the gym to shoot baskets.* ❑ VERB **shoots, shot, shoot·ing.** **–shoot′er,** NOUN.

shoot

si·lent (sī′lənt), ADJECTIVE. without any noise; quiet; still: *She tiptoed through the silent house late at night.*

space (spās), NOUN. the unlimited room or emptiness that exists in all directions: *The Earth moves through space.*

space port (spās′ pôrt), NOUN. a place where spacecraft can take off or land: *The space shuttle took off from the space port.*

space·ship (spās′ship′), NOUN. a vehicle used for flight in outer space; spacecraft.

spell·ing (spel′ing), NOUN. the act or skill of writing or saying the letters of a word in order: *I need to work on my spelling.*

storm (stôrm), NOUN. a strong wind, usually with heavy rain, snow, or hail. Some storms have thunder and lightning.

a	hat	ė	term	ô	order	ch	child		a in about
ā	age	i	it	oi	oil	ng	long		e in taken
ä	far	ī	ice	ou	out	sh	she	ə	i in pencil
â	care	o	hot	u	cup	th	thin		o in lemon
e	let	ō	open	ů	put	ᴛʜ	then		u in circus
ē	equal	ò	saw	ü	rule	zh	measure		

sug·ges·tion (səg jes′chən *or* sə jes′chən), NOUN. something proposed as an idea: *The songs were excellent suggestions.*

sum·mer (sum′ər), NOUN. the warmest season of the year, between spring and autumn.

sus·pend (sə spend′), VERB. to hang something by fastening it to something above: *The lamp was suspended from the ceiling.* ❑ VERB **sus·pends, sus·pend·ed, sus·pend·ing.**

Tt

tech·nique (tek nēk′), NOUN. a special method or system used to do something. ❑ PLURAL **tech·niques.**

thou·sand (thou′znd), NOUN OR ADJECTIVE. ten hundred; 1,000: *There were thousands of people at the concert.*

tor·na·do (tôr nā′dō), NOUN. a very violent and destructive windstorm with winds as high as 300 miles per hour; twister. A tornado extends down from a mass of dark clouds as a twisting funnel and moves across the land in a narrow path. ❑ PLURAL **tor·na·does** or **tor·na·dos.**

tornado

tour·ist (tür′ist), NOUN. someone traveling for pleasure: *Each year many tourists go to Canada.*

trace (trās), VERB. to copy by following the lines of something with a pencil or pen: *Put thin paper over the map and trace it.* ❑ VERB **trac·es, traced, trac·ing.**

tra·di·tion·al (trə dish′ə nəl), ADJECTIVE. handed down from adults to children: *Shaking hands when you meet is a traditional custom.* **–tra·di·tion·al·ly,** ADVERB.

trap (trap), NOUN. a device for catching animals: *The mouse was caught in a trap.*

trou·ble (trub′əl), NOUN. something that upsets, bothers, or worries you, or that gives you pain: *The trouble began when our car broke down in a storm.*

U u

un·der·ground (un′dər ground′), ADVERB. beneath the surface of the ground: *Most miners work underground.*

V v

va·ca·tion (vā kā′shən), NOUN. a time when you are not at school or at work: *Our family took a long vacation last year.*

vis·it (viz′it), VERB. to go to see someone and spend some time there: *I visit my friend every week.* ❑ VERB **vis·its, vis·it·ed, vis·it·ing.**

vol·can·ic (vol kan′ik), ADJECTIVE. of, about, or caused by a volcano: *They feared a volcanic eruption which would cause steam and ashes to flow down the mountain.*

vul·ner·a·ble (vul′ nər ə bəl), ADJECTIVE. easily harmed; capable of being wounded or injured: *Very old people are vulnerable to some kinds of sickness.*

a	hat	ė	term	ô	order	ch	child		a in about
ā	age	i	it	oi	oil	ng	long		e in taken
ä	far	ī	ice	ou	out	sh	she	ə	i in pencil
â	care	o	hot	u	cup	th	thin		o in lemon
e	let	ō	open	ù	put	ᴛʜ	then		u in circus
ē	equal	ò	saw	ü	rule	zh	measure		

W w

warn•ing (wôr′ning), NOUN. something that warns; notice given in advance: *We were given many warnings about the bad weather.*

warning

wealth (welth), NOUN. a large quantity; riches: *The king shared his great wealth with the kingdom.*

west (west), NOUN. the direction of the sunset.

wrecked (rekt), ADJECTIVE. completely destroyed or ruined: *The storm left a trail of wrecked homes, cars, and trees.*

a	hat	ė	term	ô	order	ch	child	⎧ a in about
ā	age	i	it	oi	oil	ng	long	⎪ e in taken
ä	far	ī	ice	ou	out	sh	she	ə ⎨ i in pencil
â	care	o	hot	u	cup	th	thin	⎪ o in lemon
e	let	ō	open	ù	put	ŦH	then	⎩ u in circus
ē	equal	ò	saw	ü	rule	zh	measure	

Acknowledgments

Text

Page 14: From *Arnie Goes to Camp* by Nancy Carlson. Copyright © 1988 by Nancy Carlson. Reprinted by permission of Viking Kestrel, a division of Penguin Putnam, Inc.

Page 16: *How I Spent My Summer Vacation* by Mark Teague. Copyright © 1995 by Mark Teague. Reprinted by arrangement with Crown Publishers, Inc.

Page 39: "The Picture Place," from *Flights of Fancy and Other Poems* by Myra Cohn Livingston. Copyright © 1994 by Myra Cohn Livingston. Reprinted by permission.

Page 40: From *Three Up a Tree* by James Marshall. Copyright © 1986 by James Marshall. Reprinted by permission of Dial Books for Young Readers, a division of Penguin Putnam, Inc.

Page 42: *Goldilocks and the Three Bears* by James Marshall. Copyright © 1988 by James Marshall. Reprinted by permission of Dial Books for Young Readers, a division of Penguin Putnam, Inc.

Page 66: Excerpts from "American Black Bears" from *Bears* by Helen Gilks. Copyright © 1993 by Helen Gilks. Reprinted by permission.

Page 68: "A Cowboy's Rope," from *The Cowboy's Handbook* by Tod Cody. Copyright © 1996 by Breslich & Foss.

Page 70: Text from *Anthony Reynoso: Born to Rope* by Martha Cooper and Ginger Gordon. Text copyright © 1996 by Ginger Gordon. Reprinted by permission of Clarion Books/ Houghton Mifflin Company. All rights reserved.

Page 87: Excepts from *Cowboy* by David H. Murdoch. Copyright © 2000 by DK Publishing. Reprinted by permission.

Page 90: From *Herbie Jones* by Suzy Kline. Copyright © 1985 by Suzy Kline. Reprinted by permission of G. P. Putnam's Sons, a division of Penguin Putnam, Inc.

Page 92: From *Herbie Jones Reader's Theater* by Suzy Kline. Text copyright © 1992 by Suzy Kline. Reprinted by permission of G. P. Putnam's Sons, a division of Penguin Putnam, Inc.

Page 108: "What Are Viruses?" from *Bacteria and Viruses* by Leslie Jean Le Master. Copyright © 1985 by Regensteiner Publishing Enterprises, Inc. Reprinted by permission.

Page 110: From *Because You're Lucky* by Irene Smalls. Illustrated by Michael Hays. Text copyright © 1997 by Irene Smalls. Illustrations copyright © 1997 by Michael Hays. Reprinted by permission of Little, Brown and Company.

Page 112: *Allie's Basketball Dream* by Barbara E. Barber. Illustrated by Darryl Ligasan. Text copyright © 1996 by Barbara E. Barber. Illustrations copyright © 1996 by Darryl Ligasan. Reprinted by permission of Lee & Low Books Inc.

Page 131: Reprinted courtesy of *Sports Illustrated for Kids* from the January 1998 edition. Copyright © 2001, Time, Inc. "SWISH!" by Andrea N. Whittaker. All rights reserved.

Page 134: "My Brother Is as Generous as Anyone Could Be" from *Something Big Has Been Here* by Jack Prelutsky. Text copyright © 1990 by Jack Prelutsky. Used by permission of HarperCollins Publishers.

Page 135: "Summer Vacation" from *My Daddy Is a Cool Dude and Other Poems* by Karama Fufuka. Text copyright © 1975 by Karama Fufuka. Reprinted by permission of Dial Books for Young Readers, a division of Penguin Putnam, Inc.

Page 136: "Poem" from *Collected Poems* by Langston Hughes. Copyright © 1994 by the Estate of Langston Hughes. Reprinted by permission of Alfred A. Knopf, Inc.

Page 136: "Watering/Regar" from *Gathering the Sun* by Alma Flor Ada. English translation by Rosa Zubizarreta. Text copyright © 1997 by Alma Flor Ada. Used by permission of HarperCollins Publishers.

Page 137: "August afternoon" from *Open the Door* by Marion Edey. Reprinted with the permission of Atheneum Books for Young Readers, an imprint of Simon & Schuster Children's Publishing Division from *Open the Door* by Marion Edey and Dorothy Grider (Charles Scribner's Sons, NY, 1949).

Page 144: From *What's Inside of Plants?* by Herbert S. Zim. New York: William Morrow & Company, Inc. 1952, pp. 4–5.

Page 146: *Fly Traps! Plants That Bite Back* by Martin Jenkins. Copyright © 1996 by Martin Jenkins. Published by Candlewick Press, Cambridge, MA. Reprinted by permission of Walker Books Limited, London.

Page 165: Adapted from "Can You Catch Flies?" by Rhonda Lucas Donald. Illustration by Tan Branch Graphics. Text copyright © 1996 by the National Wildlife Federation. Illustration copyright © 1996 by Tan Branch Graphics. Text reprinted from the April 1996 issue of *Ranger Rick Magazine* with the permission of the publisher, the National Wildlife Federation.

Page 168: From *The Willow Umbrella* by Christine Widman. Text copyright © 1993 Christine Widman. Reprinted with the permission of Simon & Schuster Books for Young Readers, an imprint of Simon & Schuster Children's Publishing Division.

Page 169: From *Roger's Umbrella* by Daniel M. Pinkwater. Illustrated by James Marshall. Copyright © 1982 by Daniel M. Pinkwater. Reprinted by permission of Dutton, a division of Penguin Putnam, Inc.

Page 170: *Guys from Space* by Daniel Pinkwater. Copyright © 1989 by Daniel Pinkwater. Reprinted by permission of Atheneum Books for Young Readers, Simon & Schuster Children's Publishing Division.

Page 186: Excerpt from *Movie Magic* by Anne Cottringer. Copyright © 1999 by DK Publishing. Reprinted by permission.

Page 188: From *Weather* by Martha Ryan. Reprinted by permission of Grolier Publishing Company.

Page 190: *Tornado Alert* by Franklyn M. Branley. Text copyright © 1988 by Franklyn M. Branley. Reprinted by permission of HarperCollins Publishers.

Page 206: Excerpts from "Myths About Tornadoes" in *Kids Discover*, Vol. 6, Issue 6, June/July 1996. Copyright © 1996 by *Kids Discover*. Reprinted by permission.

Page 208: From "My Favorite Sharks" by Don Reed from *Boys' Life* Magazine, June 1993. Reprinted by permission of Don C. Reed.

Page 210: *Danger—Icebergs!* by Roma Gans. Text copyright © 1987 by Roma Gans. Reprinted by permission of HarperCollins Publishers.

Page 224: From "Glacier Trek" by Alan Macek as told to Vivien Bowers from *Ranger Rick*, Vol. 31, No. 8, August 1997. Used by permission of Vivien Bowers.

Page 226: From *Discovering Sea Birds* by Anthony Wharton. Artwork by Wendy Meadway. First published in 1987 by Wayland Publishers. Reprinted by permission of Wayland Publishers Ltd., East Sussex, England.

Page 228: *Nights of the Pufflings* by Bruce McMillan. Copyright © 1995 by Bruce McMillan. Reprinted by permission of Houghton Mifflin Company. All rights reserved.

Page 244: "You Don't Need a Knife or Fork When You're a Spoonbill!" by Cynthia Berger. Reprinted from the June 2000 issue of *Ranger Rick* magazine, with the permission of the publisher, the National Wildlife Federation. Copyright © 2000 by the National Wildlife Federation.

Page 248: "Clouds" from *In the Woods, in the Meadow, in the Sky* by Aileen Fisher. Copyright © 1965 by Aileen Fisher. Copyright renewed 1993 by Aileen Fisher. Reprinted by permission of Marian Reiner for the author.

Page 250: "Laughing Tomatoes" from *Laughing Tomatoes and Other Spring Poems* by Francisco X. Alarcón. Reprinted with permission of the publisher, Children's Book Press, San Francisco, CA. Copyright © 1997 by Francisco X. Alarcón.

Page 251: "Fishes' Evening Song" from *Whispering and Other Things*, published by Alfred A. Knopf. Copyright © 1967 by Dahlov Ipcar. Reprinted by permission of McIntosh and Otis, Inc.

Page 258: From *Cartooning for Kids* by Carol Lea Benjamin. Copyright © 1982 by Carol Lea Benjamin. Reprinted by permission of the author.

Page 260: From *What Do Authors Do?* by Eileen Christelow. Text and illustrations copyright © 1995 by Eileen Christelow. All rights reserved. Reprinted by permission of Clarion Books/Houghton Mifflin Company.

Page 281: From "Amazing Animal Senses" by Tina Adler. Copyright © 2000 by *National Geographic World*, Used by permission of NGS Images.

Page 284: Excerpts from *The Blue Hill Meadows*, text copyright © 1997 by Cynthia Rylant, used with permission of Harcourt, Inc.

Page 286: *Tops and Bottoms* by Janet Stevens. Copyright © 1995 by Janet Stevens. Reprinted by permission of Harcourt Brace & Company.

Page 308: "Food from Plants" from *Plants* by David Burnie. Copyright © 1989 by Alfred A. Knopf. Reprinted by permission.

Page 310: From *Puppy Training and Critters, Too!* by Judy Petersen-Fleming and Bill Fleming. Copyright © 1996 by Judy Petersen-Fleming and Bill Fleming. Used by permission of HarperCollins Publishers.

Page 312: Excerpt from *Mom's Best Friend* by Sally Alexander. Text copyright © 1992 by Sally Alexander. All rights reserved. Reprinted by permission of the author and Book Stop Literary Agency.

Page 326: "Louis' Quest" from *Louis Braille: Bringer of Hope to the Blind*, by Patricia Lantier and Beverley Birch. Copyright © 1989 by Exley Publications, Ltd. Reprinted by permission.

Page 328: From *A Net of Stars* by Jennifer Richard Jacobson. Copyright © 1998 by Jennifer Richard Jacobson. Reprinted by permission of Dial Books for Young Readers, a division of Penguin Putnam, Inc.

Page 330: *Brave as a Mountain Lion* by Ann Herbert Scott. Text copyright © 1996 by Ann Herbert Scott. Illustrations copyright © 1996 by Glo Coalson. All rights reserved. Reprinted by permission of Clarion Books/Houghton Mifflin Co.

Page 350: "Spiders" Experiment from *Avocado Elementary School Website* by Carmen Johnson and Carol Ann Delancy, Avocado Elementary School, Homestead, Florida. Reprinted by permission.

Page 352: From *Mimi's Tutu* by Tynia Thomassie. Copyright © 1996 by Tynia Thomassie. Reprinted by permission of Scholastic, Inc.

Page 354: *Your Dad Was Just Like You* by Dolores Johnson. Copyright © 1993 by Dolores Johnson. Reprinted by permission of Atheneum Books for Young Readers, Simon & Schuster Children's Publishing Division.

Page 372: Excerpt from "Games and Sports" from *People* by Andrew Langley. Copyright © 1989 by Gareth Stevens Children's Books. Reprinted by permission.

Page 374: "The Steam Shovel" from *Story-Teller Poems* by Rowena Bennett.

Artists

Cover: Daniel Craig

Pages 14–15: Harry Roolaart

Pages 16–38: Mark Teague

Page 39: Diane Bigda

Pages 40–65: James Marshall

Pages 66–67: Andew Bale

Pages 68–69: Jeff Meyer

Pages 70–86: Ruta Daugavieties

Pages 90–107: Don Stewart

Pages 108–109: Barry Gott

Pages 112–130: Darryl Ligasan

Pages 134–137: John Sandford

Pages 138–139: Jo Ann Adinolfi

Pages 140–141: Tony Klassen

Pages 144–145: Marty Blake

Pages 146–164: David Parkins

Pages 168–169: Franklin Hammond

Pages 170–185: Daniel Pinkwater

Pages 188–205: Joel Spector

Pages 206–207: Brucie Rosch

Pages 208–209: Larry Day

Pages 212–221: Ebet Dudley

Pages 226–227 (Inset): Wendy Meadway

Pages 248–251: Lee Lee Brazeal

Pages 252–253: Eileen Hine

Pages 254–255: Tony Klassen

Pages 256–257: Mike Reed

Pages 258–259 (Inset): Carol Lea Benjamin

Pages 260–280: Eileen Christelow

Pages 284–285: Susan Leopold

Pages 286–307: Janet Stevens

Pages 310–311: Don Stewart

Pages 326–327: Stephanie Carter

Pages 328–329: Joel Spector

Pages 330–348: Glo Coalson

Pages 350–351 (Web Art): Tony Klassen

Pages 352–353: Gabriela Dellosso

Pages 354–371: Dolores Johnson

Pages 374–377: Darryl Ligasan

Pages 378–379: Mark Betcher

Pages 380–381: Tony Klassen

Photographs

Every effort has been made to secure permission and provide appropriate credit for photographic material. The publisher deeply regrets any omission and pledges to correct errors called to their attention in subsequent editions.

Unless otherwise acknowledged, all photographs are the property of Scott Foresman, a division of Pearson Education. Page abbreviations are as follows: (t) top, (b) bottom, (l) left, (r) right, (ins) inset, (s) spot, (bk) background.

Page 11: Sharon Hoogstraten

Pages 12–13: Ed Honowitz/Tony Stone Images

Page 37: Richard Hutchings for Scott Foresman

Page 64: Courtesy Houghton Mifflin Co.

Pages 71–84: Martha Cooper

Page 85: (T) Martha Cooper; (B) Jim Norman

Page 87: (R) PhotoDisc; (BR) Bob Langrish

Page 88: (CL) Hutchinson Library; (CR) © DK Picture Library

Page 89: (TR), (CR), (BR), (BC) Bob Langrish/© DK Picture Library

Page 106: Courtesy Suzy Kline, Photographer: Dalla Valle (Inset)

Pages 106–107, 110–111: Sharon Hoogstraten

Page 109: (TC), (TR), (CR) American Society of Microbiology

Page 129: Richard Hutchings for Scott Foresman

Pages 131–132: Manny Millan/Sports Illustrated

Page 133: (B) Manny Millan/Sports Illustrated; (BKGRD) Nathaniel S. Butler/NBA/Sports Illustrated; (T-INSET) Manny Millan/Sports Illustrated

Pages 142–143: T. Davis/W. Dilendulo/Tony Stone Images

Page 165: John Netherton

Page 184: Kathy McLaughlin

Page 186: (TL), (CL) Planet Earth Pictures; (BL) Richard Berenholtz/Stock Market; (BR) Geoff Brightling/Evolution FX

Page 187: (TR), (CR) Geoff Brightling/Evolution FX; (B) © DK Picture Library

Page 188: (INSET) NASA

Page 191: Superstock

Page 193: Beryl Bidwell/Tony Stone Images

Page 196: Charles Doswell/Tony Stone Images

Page 198: (B) Spencer Tirey/Liaison Network; (TL, TR) AP/Wide World

Page 199: David J. Sams/Tony Stone Images

Page 200: NASA

Pages 204 (TL), **205:** (TR) PhotoDisc

Pages 210–211: Price/OSF/Animals Animals

Page 212: David Muench/Tony Stone Images

Page 216: Corbis/UPI/Bettmann

Pages 218–219: John Beatty/Tony Stone Images

Page 222: Special Collections, Milbank Memorial Library, Teachers College, Columbia University

Pages 226–227: © IFA/West Stock

Pages 228–243: Bruce McMillan

Page 242: (B) Benner McGee

Page 244: (R) Joe McDonald

Page 245: (TR) Arthur Morris/Birds As Art

Page 246: (TL) Lisa Husar/DRK Photo; (TR, B) Donald M. Jones; (C) Stephen J. Krasemann/DRK Photo

Page 247: (T) Donald M. Jones; (BR) John Netherton/Oxford Scientific Films

Pages 258–259: Sharon Hoogstraten (Backgrounds)

Page 281: (BR) J. Brown/OSF/Animals Animals/Earth Scenes

Page 282: (CR) Michio Hoshino/Minden Pictures; (BL) Robert Pearcy/Animals Animals/Earth Scenes; (BR) Konrad Wothe/Minden Pictures

Page 283: (BL) Flip Nicklin/Minden Pictures; (BR) Carol J. Kaelson/Animals Animals/ Earth Scenes

Pages 305–306: Courtesy Janet Stevens

Page 308: (BL, BR, R) © DK Picture Library

Page 309: (TL, TR, CR, BL, BR) © DK Picture Library

Pages 312–323: George Ancona

Page 324: (T) Courtesy Sally Hobart Alexander; (B) Courtesy George Ancona

Page 348: Lawrence Migdale for Scott Foresman

Page 351: (T) Richard Shiell/Animals Animals/Earth Scenes; (C) Bruce MacDonald/ Animals Animals/Earth Scenes; (B) Joe MacDonald/Bruce Coleman Inc.

Page 370: Courtesy Dolores Johnson

Page 372: (T, B) © Bettmann/Corbis; (C) © Reuters NewMedia Inc./Corbis

Page 373: (T) © Pablo San Juan/Corbis; (C) © Bettmann/Corbis; (BL) © Paul A. Souders/Corbis; (BR) © AFP/Corbis

Glossary

The contents of the glossary have been adapted from *Beginning Dictionary,* copyright © 1999, Scott Foresman and Company.